G000128482

The HIDDEN PLACES *of* SURREY

Edited by
Sean Connolly

© Travel Publishing Ltd. 1998

Published by:
Travel Publishing Ltd
7a Apollo House, Calleva Park
Aldermaston, Berks, RG7 8TN

ISBN 1-902-00708-5
© Travel Publishing Ltd 1998

First Published: *1993*
Second Edition: *1995*
Third Edition: *1998*

Regional Titles in the Hidden Places Series:

Channel Islands
Cheshire
Cornwall
Devon
Dorset, Hants & Isle of Wight
Gloucestershire
Heart of England
Kent
Lake District & Cumbria
Lancashire
Norfolk
Northeast Yorkshire
Northumberland & Durham
Nottinghamshire
Peak District
Potteries
Somerset
South East
South Wales
Suffolk
Surrey
Sussex
Thames & Chilterns
Welsh Borders
Wiltshire
Yorkshire Dales

National Titles in the Hidden Places Series:

England
Ireland
Scotland
Wales

Printing by: Nuffield Press, Abingdon

Cartography by: Estates Publications, Tenterden, Kent

Line Drawings: Sarah Bird

Editor: Sean Connolly

Cover : Clare Hackney

Born in 1961, Clare was educated at West Surrey College of Art and Design as well as studying at Kingston University. She runs her own private water-colour school based in Surrey and has exhibited both in the UK and internationally. The cover is taken from an original water-colour of the village of Outwood.

All information is included by the publishers in good faith and is believed to be correct at the time of going to press. No responsibility can be accepted for errors.

This book is sold subject to the condition that it shall not by way of trade or otherwise be lent, re-sold, hired out, or otherwise circulated without the publisher's prior consent in any form of binding or cover other than that which it is published and without similar condition including this condition being imposed on the subsequent purchase.

Foreword

The Hidden Places series is a collection of easy to use travel guides taking you, in this instance, on a relaxed but informative tour through Surrey - a county rich in heritage and unexpectedly endowed with natural beauty and charming picturesque villages. Our books contain a wealth of interesting information on the history, the countryside, the towns and villages and the more established places of interest in the county. But they also promote the more secluded and little known visitor attractions and places to stay, eat and drink many of which are easy to miss unless you know exactly where you are going.

We include hotels, inns, restaurants, public houses, teashops, various types of accommodation, historic houses, museums, gardens, garden centres, craft centres and many other attractions throughout Surrey. Most places have an attractive line drawing and are cross-referenced to coloured maps found at the rear of the book. We do not award merit marks or rankings but concentrate on describing the more interesting, unusual or unique features of each place with the aim of making the reader's stay in the local area an enjoyable and stimulating experience.

Whether you are visiting Surrey for business or pleasure or in fact are living in the county we do hope that you enjoy reading and using this book. We are always interested in what readers think of places covered (or not covered) in our guides so please do not hesitate to use the reader reaction forms provided to give us your considered comments. We also welcome any general comments which will help us improve the guides themselves. Finally if you are planning to visit any other corner of the British Isles we would like to refer you to the list of other ***Hidden Places*** titles to be found at the rear of the book.

Contents

CHAPTER ONE
Northeast Surrey

Kew Gardens Palm House

Chapter 1 - Area Covered

For precise location of places please refer to the colour maps found at the rear of the book.

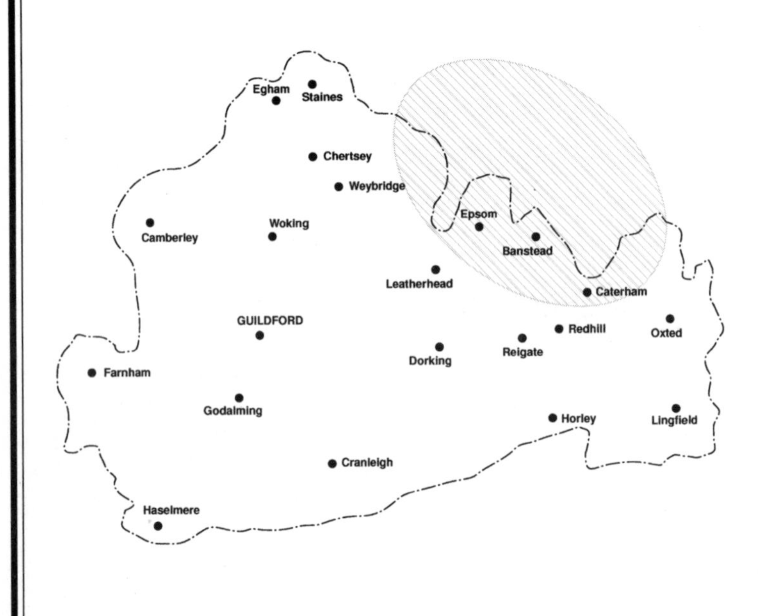

1
Northeast Surrey

Introduction

Surrey has always had to define itself in relation to London, and the county as a whole tends to typify what most people would describe as the "commuter belt". The implication is that Surrey is nothing more than a collection of anonymous suburbs extending south and west from the capital, offering the more well-off the chance to have lawns to mow but with not much more in the way of nature or history.

The great swathe of Surrey that lies due south of London, with the M25 as its southern border, takes this preconception to the extreme. Indeed much of what had originally been - and which steadfastly continues to consider itself - Surrey was absorbed by London in the boundary changes of 1965. Growing conurbations such as Kingston and Croydon house and employ thousands, and rail lines and major roads fan through the area from London.

Yet, as so often is the case, received wisdom includes more than its share of ignorance. This northeast corner of Surrey is full of historical areas, some well known and others that are truly hidden gems. Great houses, as well as royal and Episcopal palaces, were built here from medieval times, and many villages have evidence of Saxon, Celtic, roman and even late Stone Ages settlements. And the countryside in this stretch of Surrey is as varied as nearly anywhere in the south of England. From the well-maintained oases of Kew Gardens to the Down and Weald uplands to the south, there are parks, greens, heaths, commons and open land. And in most of the area covered by this chapter the most prominent sounds to be heard are not lawnmowers and strimmers but birdsong, the click of a cricket bat or the crackle of a log fire burning in a country pub.

Kingston

Kingston upon Thames is the administrative centre of Surrey, so it is not surprising that it should have more than its share of busy offices charged with the job of keeping the governmental wheels oiled and in good order. In fact, the first impression most people have of Kingston is of high-rise office blocks and its famous by-pass, giving it the sense of being totally urbanised and something of a modern creation.

The conclusion is misleading, since Kingston is a thriving market town and has been since the Middle Ages. The trick with Kingston is to know what to look for, and not to be put off by some of the less edifying modern elements. The Guildhall, built in 1935, is solid and functional, but near it is the ***Coronation Stone***, which is said to have been used in the crowning of at least six Saxon kings.

Other historians, perhaps less romantic, dispute the function of the stone, arguing that the town's name does not refer to the "king's stone" - evidence used in the coronation theory - but that it was an estate belonging to the king. Nevertheless, records show that Kingston was a prosperous town in Anglo-Saxon times, regardless of whether the monarchs assumed office there.

The river has been crossed by a bridge since medieval times and the present bridge was built in 1825. Regular street markets have been held on a site by the bridge since the 17th century, and stalls do good trade in flowers, fruit and vegetables. Kingston parish church was completely rebuilt in neo-Gothic style in the 19th century, but its interior still contains many medieval monuments. On the London Road, however, is a real medieval relic - the chapel of ***St Mary Magdalene***, which dates from the 14th century.

The district of Coombe, to the east of Kingston, was rebuilt by prosperous Victorians. Large houses, built in a variety of architectural styles, came to symbolise the solid financial standing of their owners. It is unfortunate that few of these houses survive apart from their impressive gate lodges, but there are a few exceptions such as ***Coombe Pines*** in Warren Cutting. John Galsworthy began the development of Coombe Hill, and two of his own houses survive - ***Coombe Leigh***, which is now a convent, and ***Coombe Ridge***, today a school. Galsworthy's son was the famous novelist and set Soames Forsyte's house in Coombe.

Around Kingston

Twickenham *Map 1 ref G2*

4 miles N of Kingston on the A310

Lying on the west side of the Thames just a few miles north of Hampton Court Palace, Twickenham is a thriving community that makes the most of its riverside setting. Perhaps more than anything else Twickenham is renowned as the headquarters of Rugby Union Football in Britain, a role it has played since 1907. The recently rebuilt stadium - *"Twickers"* to some of its dearest stalwarts - plays host to England home internationals as well as the annual Varsity match between Oxford and Cambridge. Admission to the ***Museum of Rugby*** allows visitors to savour the history and atmosphere of the sport. Running through the players tunnel is enough to get many people's blood rushing, and the museum provides a full account of Twickenham right up to its latest renovations.

A number of fine old houses are dotted through the heart of Twickenham. Montpelier Row and Sion Row are wonderfully preserved terraces dating from the 18th century. Those eager to pursue other historical associations from that era can find the tomb of the poet Alexander Pope in the Twickenham churchyard.

At ***Strawberry Hill***, just to the south of Twickenham, is a Gothic Revival villa built between 1750 and 1776 for the author Horace Walpole. The motley assortment of architectural styles has led to its description as "part of a church, a castle, a monastery or a mansion". Strawberry Hill is now St Mary's University College, a teachers' training college, but it is open to the public.

Orleans House and Gallery, which houses one of London's finest art collections outside of London's national collections, enjoys an enviable location in a woodland garden on the Riverside between Twickenham and Richmond. On the opposite riverbank is Ham House, with its extensive grounds, while next door is the Palladian villa of Marble Hill House.

This choice setting, beside one of the loveliest curves of the River Thames, inspired James Johnston, Joint Secretary of State for Scotland under King William III, to have a stately home built here. The architect was John James, who later rebuilt Twickenham Parish Church. Johnston was a great favourite of Queen Caroline, wife of King George II, and he had the Octagon, originally designed as a garden pavilion, added to the house in 1720 in honour of a visit by Queen Caroline. The House acquired its present name from its most famous resident, Louis Philippe, Duc d'Orleans, who lived here from 1815 until 1817 during his exile from Napoleonic France. He later ruled as King of the French from 1830 to 1848.

Orleans House & Gallery

Most of Orleans House was demolished in 1926 and 1927 but the Octagon and two wings were saved by the Hon. Mrs Levy, later the Hon. Mrs Ionides. The property, along with the Ionides collection of paintings and prints of the locality, were bequeathed to the local Borough on her death in 1962 to become a public gallery.

Jane Dalton and Rachel Tranter, the Gallery curator and assistant curator respectively, oversee the London Borough of Richmond upon Thames Art Collection, which comprises almost 2,000 pictures dating from the early eighteenth century to the present day. In addition they organise a series of lectures and exhibitions highlighting modern trends, crafts, multimedia artists and imaginative activities to kindle the artistic flame. *Orleans House and Gallery, Riverside, Twickenham TW1 3DJ Tel: 0181 892 0221, Fax: 0181 744 0501*

Richmond

Map1 ref G1

5 miles N of Kingston on the A307

Although a sizeable commercial centre with a wide range of high street chains and department stores, Richmond retains a distinct sense of its rich and varied history. Its twin blessings - a lovely riverside setting along a sweeping curve of the Thames and the extensive ***Richmond Park*** - act as counterpoints to the occasionally heavy traffic and the sound of planes approaching Heathrow Airport.

A good place to get acquainted with old Richmond is ***Richmond Green***, a genuine village green that is hardly surpassed in all of Greater London. Handsome houses, built in the17th and 18th centuries, flank the southwest and southeast edges of the green. The southwest side has an older, and more royal, history. It was the site of Richmond Palace, built in the 12th century and passing into royal possession in 1125, when it was known as Shene Palace. The palace was destroyed by Richard II in 1394 but subsequent kings had it rebuilt in stages. The site, right by the green, made it an ideal spot for organising jousting tournaments. The rebuilding and extensions reached their peak under Henry VII, who renamed the palace after his Yorkshire earldom. Elizabeth I died in the palace in 1603. Sadly, very little of the palace survives as it was a victim of the turbulent Commonwealth upheavals in the 17th century. Look for the only surviving element - the brick gatehouse - beside the green.

Richmond Theatre

Just off the northeast flank of the green is the ***Richmond Theatre***, an imposing Victorian building with an elaborate frontage facing the street. It is a showcase for excellent theatrical productions. The combination of the repertoire and the lovely setting attracts a number of renowned actors.

The Burnt Chair is a small, welcoming restaurant in one of the narrow lanes that run off Richmond Green. This location is worth noting, because the Richmond Theatre is just around the corner and you might find yourself at the next table to Tom Conti, Edward Woodward or other thespians keen to recharge their batteries after a draining rehearsal. Chef-proprietor Weenson Oo presides over a cuisine that features the best of French and English cooking - there is room on the menu for black pudding as well as soufflé - and there

The Burnt Chair

are some rewarding surprises, such as salmon tandoori, for the adventurous. But you needn't suspect that this adventurousness extends as far as well-done seating: the restaurant was christened when the chef put a stockpot down on a kitchen chair, leaving it charred. A fine cheese board, again featuring English and French choices, and a thoughtful wine list round off an excellent dining experience. *The Burnt Chair, 5 Duke Street, Richmond, Surrey TW9 1HP Tel: 0181 940 9488*

Richmond Riverside, a redevelopment scheme dating from the late 1980s, stretches along the Thames. Pastiche Georgian buildings, complete with columns, cupolas and facades, house offices and commercial premises. Among the modern buildings, however, there remain a few of the original Georgian and Victorian houses, including the narrow, three-storey ***Heron House***, where Lady Hamilton and her daughter Horatia came to live soon after the Battle of Trafalgar. The riverside walk ends at ***Richmond Bridge***, a handsome five-arched structure built of Purbeck stone in 1777 and widened in the 1930s. It is the oldest extant bridge spanning the Thames in London.

Richmond's Old Town Hall, set somewhat back from the new developments at Richmond Bridge, is the home of the ***Museum of Richmond***, a fascinating privately run museum which provides a unique perspective on Richmond's history and special significance in English life. The Museum's permanent displays chronicle the story of Richmond, Ham, Petersham and Kew - communities that grew

Museum of Richmond

and prospered because of their choice location along the Thames downstream from Hampton Court. For centuries the area has been a centre of fashion, the arts and the intellect. The collections of the Museum of Richmond concentrate on different aspects of this history, detailing the rich heritage from prehistoric times through to the present.

Special features and detailed models focus on some of the most noteworthy buildings, such as the ***Charterhouse of Shene***, which was the largest Carthusian Monastery in England. The information about Richmond Palace is a bit of English history in microcosm. Built by Henry VII - and like the town named after his Yorkshire Earldom in 1501 - the Palace was later a favourite home of Elizabeth I. It was from here that she issued orders to defeat the Spanish Armada in 1588.

A number of displays concentrate on the luminaries who have made Richmond their home over the years. Among the roll call of the Great and the Good are Sir Robert Walpole, Sir Joshua Reynolds, Lady Emma Hamilton, George Eliot, Virginia Woolf, Gustav Holst and Bertrand Russell.

Temporary exhibitions, one of the most popular features of the museum, concentrate on subjects of local interest, and recent topics have included Georgian wallpapers, the 'home front' in Richmond, Richmond Ice Rink, training ground for some of Britain's best figure skaters and local artists and writers such as Spencer Gore, Thomas Rowlandson and Virginia Woolf. *Museum of Richmond, Old Town Hall, Whittaker Avenue, Richmond, Surrey TW9 1TP Tel: 0181 332 1141*

The occasionally steep climb of ***Richmond Hill*** leads southwards and upwards from the centre of Richmond. The view from the top, at Richmond Terrace, makes the climb worth it. The Thames lies below, sweeping in majestic curves to the west through wooded countryside. Turner and Reynolds are among the many artists who have tried to capture the essence of this scene, which takes in six counties. A little further up the hill is the entrance to ***Richmond Park***, some 2,400 acres of open land where deer roam. Set amidst this coppiced woodland are several landscaped plantations noted for their azaleas and rhododendrons. The land achieved park status under Charles I.

Occupying a tranquil location on the peaceful banks of the Thames south of Richmond is ***Ham House***, one of the best examples of a Stuart stately home in the country. Ham House was built in 1610 for one of James I's courtiers and in 1626 it passed to William Murray, a close friend of Charles II and later made the first Earl of Dysart. It was Murray, and to an even greater extent his daughter

Ham House

Elizabeth, who gave the house its abiding character. Outside it is well proportioned and almost austere - its handsome red brick and white-bordered exterior looks out on to spacious formal gardens. But it is the interior that captures the imagination with its imposing Great Staircase leading the visitor into a world of exuberant Baroque furnishings and a wealth of fine paintings and tapestries. The National Trust, which acquired Ham House in 1948, preserves this architectural gem, and discerning visitors are treated to a view of one of Britain's most complete collections of late seventeenth century furnishings. *Ham House, Richmond, Surrey TW10 7RS Tel: 0181 940 1950*

Kew and Kew Gardens *Map 1 ref G1*

7 miles N of Kingston off the A310

Riverside Kew, lying just a couple of miles North of Richmond, came to prominence under the early Hanoverian kings in the 18th century. High society followed royalty westward to the new palace built on this pleasant stretch of the Thames just upstream from Chiswick and Hammersmith. The new village grew around triangular Kew Green, which is still surrounded by handsome 18th century houses.

Far more important than Kew's social history, however, are the ***Royal Botanical Gardens***, which are arguably the most famous gardens in the world. Princess Augusta, mother of George III, laid out an 8 acre botanical garden on the grounds of Kew Palace in 1759. Tranquil and spacious, these gardens now occupy 300 acres and also constitute one of the most important botanical research

Kew Gardens Palm House

centres in the world. More than 50,000 species are grown in plantations and glasshouses, which themselves attract over a million visitors a year. The most famous - and oldest, built in 1848 - glasshouse is the ***Palm House***, which houses most of the known palm species. Nearby is the Waterlily House, full of tropical vines and creepers overhanging its lily pond. The newest, however, is the Prince of Wales Conservatory, which opened in 1987. It houses plants from ten different climatic zones, from arid desert to tropical rainforest.

Several of the buildings constructed for Princess Augusta's amusement still stand in the grounds of the garden, but Kew also houses

Britain's smallest royal residence. The three-storey ***Kew Palace***, sometimes nicknamed the Dutch House because of its Flemish-bond brickwork, measures only 50 feet by 70 feet. The only king to have lived in this miniature palace was George III, confined here from1802 during his infamous madness. Behind the palace is a meticulously recreated 17th century garden, with helpful adages, such as *"this cureth ill temper"*, added to the labels identifying the herbs.

Another Kew landmark is the ***Chinese pagoda***, which was designed by Sir William Chambers who was responsible for much of the building in the gardens. The pagoda was purely for decoration, but it now serves as a practical purpose - as a navigational aid for visitors - since the ten storey octagonal structure stands 163 feet high. The bottom storey is 26 feet in diameter and 18 feet high. In each successive storey the diameter and height are reduced by one foot.

Chinese Pagoda, Kew

Mortlake

Map 4 ref H1

7 miles N of Kingston on the A205

The large brewery is most people's abiding impression of Mortlake, although it was once an attractive riverside village. Its name is said to derive from the French word mort, meaning "dead", a possible reference to the gruesome river traffic in corpses it oversaw during the years of the Black Death in the Middle Ages. Very little of that early period survives but the gothic west tower of St Mary Church was built on the orders of Henry VIII in 1548. A series of handsome 18th century houses face the river along Thames Bank, which continues north and west under Chiswick Bridge.

Wimbledon

Map 4 ref H2

3 miles N of Kingston on the A219

To most people Wimbledon is synonymous with the All-England Lawn Tennis Championships held each year at the end of June and in early July. However, the grounds of the All England Lawn Tennis and Croquet Club - the full name of the famous venue - are open throughout the year and there is still the chance for a buzz of excitement passing by the famous Centre Court stand in mid-winter. The Club also has the ***Wimbledon Lawn Tennis Museum***, which offers the chance to peruse a range of exhibits stretching from the era of long flannel trousers to tie-breaks and disputed line calls.

There is more to Wimbledon than tennis. This suburb on the southern fringes of London is worth visiting throughout the year. In fact, the Championship fortnight is probably the best time to avoid Wimbledon, since the streets are thronged with would-be spectators and there are heavy traffic jams in and out of the town.

The centre of Wimbledon, by its rail and Underground station, is a thriving commercial area, with stores lining the high street. Here, cheek by jowl with anonymous buildings dating from the 1960s, are a few gems. ***Eagle House***, just west of the imposing National Westminster bank building, was built in 1613. It takes a bit of imagination today to see how this house would have towered over its neighbours, but its Jacobean appearance, with three large bay windows by its central entrance, still conveys a harmonious grandeur. Further on, and now occupying numbers 44-45, is an interesting L-shaped house dating from the late 17th century.

From Wimbledon itself, Wimbledon High Street then climbs steeply to the west towards ***Wimbledon Village***, which has more of a boutique and bistro feel to it. Handsome residential streets lead off the High Street on its climb, and there are expansive views looking east across South London.

Marple Cottage is a small guest house located on a quiet street not far from Wimbledon High Street. As in real estate, the three most important factors in accommodation could be described as location, location and location. Marple Cottage scores on all three counts. It is handy for the All England Championships and the train and Underground connections from Wimbledon make it an ideal jumping-off point for sightseeing and shopping in the West End or forays to the country south of London. Owner Bridgeen McDermott ensures that guests feel at home, and part of her charm lies in her Donegal origins. The welcoming atmosphere must lie behind the numbers of repeat customers. The house itself, built in the early

Marple Cottage

nineteenth century, is covered in ivy, in keeping with this leafy area of southwest London. The eight rooms are furnished comfortably and feature an unobtrusive contemporary style. *Marple Cottage, 113 Woodside, Wimbledon, London SW19 7BA Tel: 0181 947 1487, 0181 879 1363*

Further above Wimbledon Village is ***Wimbledon Common***, covering more than 1,000 acres and providing one of the capital's largest areas of public access. Walking and riding trails criss-cross this bracken and tree-covered plateau. At the southwest corner is an Iron Age mound which was built as a fortification. Although given the name ***Caesar's Camp***, it cannot be linked by archaeologists to the Romans. Nevertheless, this fort does have a long history, and pottery fragments uncovered from it have been shown to date from the 3rd century BC.

New Malden

Map 4 ref H3

2 miles S of Kingston on the A2043

Occupying a position just a few miles east of Hampton Court and just south of both Richmond Park and Wimbledon Common is New Malden. Excellent road and rail connections link this neat suburb with Central London as well as points south, with the A3 lying about half a mile east of the rail station. New Malden makes a good base from which to explore the nearby sights, especially by using public transport and thereby avoiding traffic and parking problems.

There are a few surprises lurking in this corner of suburbia. Just by the church on Church Road is the red-brick ***Manor House***, dating from the late 17th century. Further along, to the northeast, is a duck pond, flanked by the Plough Inn. This pub seems modern but its core was built more than 500 years ago.

Angela Evans and her husband Anthony provide some of the most highly regarded bed and breakfast accommodation in New Malden. Although tucked away on a quiet road, their house is just a short stroll from the centre of town. The house faces on to an extensive gravel parking area. There is a feel of solid Victorian propriety

Angela Evans, 30 Presburg Road

to the exterior of the house, suggesting that it could once have been the home of one of New Malden's leading bankers or town councillors. The furnishings inside strengthen this traditional feel and there are a number of pieces of fine antique furniture on display in the public rooms and in the three bedrooms. The Evanses, however, are anything but stuffy and they ensure that guests settle in comfortably. They are also knowledgeable sources of information about New Malden and the surrounding area. *Angela Evans, 30 Presburg Road, New Malden, Surrey KT3 5AH Tel: 0181 949 4910*

Surbiton

Map 1 ref G3

3 miles W of Kingston on the A307

Surbiton is a well-heeled suburb that lies roughly a mile south of Kingston but manages to escape much of the traffic and commercial build-up that can bedevil its northern neighbour. Handsome properties and good rail connections proclaim Surbiton as the inner fringe of Surrey's noted commuter belt, and it is not hard to work out why houses should be so sought after here, given Surbiton's handiness both to London and to the south coast.

Surbiton could be described as a precursor of the "new towns" of the 20th century, and it was called Kingston New Town when it was developed in the 19th century. It even went by the name of Kingston-on-Railway when the railway arrived in 1840. Most of the public buildings date from this period of Victorian expansion and the architecture of churches such as ***St Andrew*** and ***St Matthew*** are good examples of the Gothic Revival that was so dominant at the time.

The A307, also known as the Portsmouth Road follows the course of the Thames through Surbiton, managing to provide lovely views of ***Hampton Court Park*** on the opposite bank of the river. ***Hampton Court Palace*** is itself just over a mile from the heart of Surbiton.

Pembroke Lodge Guest House is located on a quiet street in Surbiton, although it is well placed for easy road and rail access for

Pembroke Lodge Guest House

the London-Kingston-Epsom routes. The capital is only 15 minutes away by train. This convenient location, coupled with the sense of real comfort provided by proprietor Michael Fletcher, makes Pembroke Lodge a popular resting spot, so it is essential to book in advance. A handsome flagstone driveway sweeps past the well-maintained gardens that front the house; further gardens extend well behind. These are a particular love of Michael, who was also responsible for the tasteful interior decoration. The public rooms and the spacious bedrooms are tastefully appointed and have a real sense of space. Features such as colour televisions and teamakers in each room add a note of comfort, while full English and Continental breakfasts offer alternatives in the morning. *Pembroke Lodge Guest House, 35 Cranes Park, Surbiton, Surrey KT5 8AB Tel: 0181 390 0731*

Between Kingston and Croydon

Cheam *Map 4 ref H3*

5 miles E of Kingston on the A217

Roughly equidistant between Kingston and Croydon, Cheam is one of the prettier suburbs that dot this expanse where the metropolis begins to take on something of a less built up and more countrified air. Not that Cheam could be considered country anymore, as it has felt the inexorable pull of London throughout this century. It does manage to retain a green and leafy feel, however, thanks to the large plots on which many of the substantial houses have been built. Gardening is something of a passion in these parts and several homes in Cheam open their gardens as part of the National Gardens Scheme Charitable Trust.

As with so many other parts of Surrey where London has encroached, Cheam has lost much of its overtly medieval elements, but some careful detective work can lead to some pleasant surprises. ***St Dunstan Church***, built in the 1860s, is a large and uninspiring Victorian work but its courtyard contains the surviving portion of the medieval parish church - the ***Lumley Chapel***, which was originally the chancel. The remnant of a 3rd century arch leads to a former chapel and the roof inside was remodelled in 1592. A series of delightful and well-preserved brasses commemorates Cheam notables from the late 14th century to the Elizabethan period.

Despite its name, ***The Harrow Inn*** is located in Cheam, along the High Street which gives Londoners a foretaste of the country while lying just south of the great metropolis. In fact the Harrow

The Harrow Inn

Inn reflects some of the relatively recent reshaping of Cheam, as the nineteenth century village grew into a bustling town in the early part of this century. The pub was rebuilt in the 1920s to make room for the High Street, but the look of the pub suggests an earlier date, a reflection of the skill with which the builders succeeded with its timbered exterior and wood-panelled interior decor. The large bar, which has a separate no smoking area, has a good range of drinks and is popular with locals. The dining area has an extensive food menu that includes daily blackboard specials as well as the popular offerings shared by other pubs in the Big Steak group. Children are made particularly welcome with special main courses and sweets that will have parents dipping a spoon in 'just to taste'. *The Harrow Inn, High Street, Cheam, Surrey SM3 8RQ Tel: 0181 643 9969*

Carshalton *Map 4 ref I3*

6 miles E of Kingston on the A232

The heart of old Carshalton is clustered around two ornamental ponds, which lend a tranquil air to a community that in other respects has a suburban feel. Within this core are several fine old houses with grounds that are open to the public. One of them, ***Carshalton House***, was finished in 1713 for Sir John Fellowes, a governor of the South Sea Company. The house is imposing, especially when first seen on the road from Sutton. It is a solid affair of red and yellow brick standing two storeys high, with an attic storey above the cornice. The harmonious, yet restrained look of the house is exactly the effect that so appealed to architects at the time of Queen Anne. An indication of the evolution of this architectural taste is apparent in the porch, built about 50 years later, with its Corinthian columns reflecting a renewed love of Classical embellishment. Some of the rooms have excellent Rococo ornamentation. Outside is an impressive water house, a tower which blends in with the architecture of the main house. It serve a functional purpose, housing a pump which lifted water from the river into a cistern which fed the house.

Carshalton High Street, otherwise known as the A232, is the old posting road that connected Croydon and Sutton. This 'mainline' location has served ***The Greyhound Hotel*** well since it was built in the early 1700s. Dutch-style gables on its cream-coloured exterior provide further evidence of its early history, since this architectural style was popular during the reign of King William III when

The Greyhound Hotel

there was an inclination for anything Dutch. Today's Greyhound, with its welcoming bars and four comfortable bedrooms complete with colour television and telephone, is a far cry from the tavern which echoed to the sounds of cock fights and gambling in the eighteenth century. However, there is still a strong sense of history in this listed building, and manager Judy Gillis might even tell you about the ghost of the cloaked traveller who was found frozen on the doorstep one winter's night. *The Greyhound Hotel, 2 High Street, Carshalton, Surrey SM5 3PE Tel: 0181 647 1511*

Two miles south of Carshalton, on the downs, is a public park with some majestic trees. These formed part of the grounds of a stately home, ***The Mansion***, which was destroyed in an air raid in 1944. It was the home of the 12th Earl of Derby, founder of the famous horse race that bears his aristocratic name.

Beddington — *Map 4 ref I3*

2 miles W of Croydon off the A235

Croydon Airport, which was located in Beddington, closed down in 1959, leading to the development of several housing estates which tend to dominate the town. However, traces of Beddington's past are visible in its church, ***St Mary***, a large building which was probably begun in the 11th century. The local landowner, Sir Nicholas Carew, left money for rebuilding the church in the late 14th century, and the Carew Chapel bears his name. He, along with many of his descendants, are commemorated in brasses in this chapel and in the chancel of the church. Other additions to the church give it an eclectic air. One of the most attractive is the organ gallery, built in1869. The player's space is screened like a minstrel's gallery.

Croydon — *Map 4 ref I3*

9 miles E of Kingston on the A23

Looking at the high-rise flats and offices, one-way systems and traffic lights, it is hard to imagine that Croydon was not much more than a large village less than two centuries ago. That historic past seems to have been obliterated in a headlong rush to development.

Yet, as with so many other large British towns, first impressions can be deceiving. Nestling beneath some of the most modern high-rises are some much older buildings, including some brick almshouses built in 1599 and now overshadowed by their modern neighbours. More intriguingly, and certainly worth seeking out, are the remains of the ***Palace*** that was the summer residence of the Archbishops of Canterbury. The palace was built in the 11th century by Archbishop Lanfranc. It was considerably altered and expanded in subsequent centuries but remained an official residence until 1757. The Palace is now part of the Old Palace School for girls but the public can see some of the oldest surviving elements, including the Norman undercroft and the 15th century banqueting hall.

St John the Baptist Church is the largest parish church in Surrey, with a two-storey porch and fine tower. Its enormous size, putting it in a league with St Mary Redcliffe in Bristol and St Martin in Salisbury, derives from the fact that it was built largely at the archbishop's expense. The church burnt down in 1867 but was rebuilt by 1870 in a style that largely matches the earlier church. Some elements of the medieval church remain in the interior, including the large brass lectern.

Croydon also has a handsome arts complex, the ***Fairfield Halls***, which flank one edge of a modern flower-filled square in the heart of Croydon. It comprises a main concert hall, the Peggy Ashcroft Theatre, the Arnhem Art gallery and a general-purpose lounge which doubles as a banqueting hall. ***Waddon Caves***, along Alton Road, were the site of late Stone Age and Iron Age settlements, which were inhabited until the 3rd or 4th century AD.

East from Epsom

Epsom — *Map 1 ref H4*

6 miles S of Kingston off the A240

The old market and spa town of Epsom is a prosperous residential centre which lies on the edge of London's southwestern suburbs. In the early 17th century, it was observed that cattle were refusing to drink from a spring on the common above the town and subsequent tests revealed the water to be high in magnesium sulphate, a mineral believed to have highly beneficial medicinal properties. As the fashion for "taking the waters" grew towards the end of the century, wealthy people from London came in increasing numbers to sample the benefits of Epsom salts and the settlement grew from a small village to a town with its own street market, a charter for which was granted in 1685.

By the end of the 18th century, the popularity of Epsom's spa was on the decline, but by this time, the town's pleasant rural location within easy reach of the City of London was already starting to attract well-to-do business people; a number of substantial residential homes were built in and around the town during this period, several of which survive to this day. A lively street market continues to be held every Saturday in Epsom High Street, a wide and impressive thoroughfare which contains some noteworthy old buildings, including a Victorian clock tower and the part 17th century ***Waterloo House***, formerly the New Tavern.

Epsom's other main claim to fame is as a horse-racing centre. Each year in early June, the Downs to the southeast of the town take on a carnival atmosphere as tens of thousands of racing enthusiasts come to experience the annual Classic race meeting and the colourful funfair which accompanies it. Informal horse racing took place on ***Epsom Downs*** as long ago as 1683 when Charles II is said to have been in attendance. Racing was formalised in 1779 when a party of aristocratic sportsmen led by Lord Derby established a race for three year old fillies which was named after the Derbys' family home at Banstead, the Oaks; this was followed a year later by a race for all three year olds, the Derby, which was named after the founder himself, although only after he won a toss of a coin with the race's co-founder, Sir Charles Bunbury. (Had Lord Derby lost, the race would have become known as the Bunbury.) The Oaks and the Derby were a great success and soon achieved Classic status along with the St Leger at Doncaster, the earliest to be established in 1776, and the 1000 Guineas and 2000 Guineas at Newmarket, established in 1814 and 1809 respectively.

The Amato takes its name from the 1838 Derby winner and the unofficial link with the great race is still maintained proudly at this popular pub on a small lane in Epsom. The Amato has a history of forecasting the Derby winner - three in the last four years - so there's

The Amato

an especially good reason for visiting in early June. The insiders' knowledge seems to come from the gypsies who visit the pub each year just before the big race. Tom Inglis has been landlord here for 12 years and has a good following, and not just for his racing tips. He serves a good range of real ales and beers and the Sunday lunch trade is brisk - make sure to book to ensure a table for a fortifying meal. The garden is also an attraction, whether you're having some food, studying the racing form or simply enjoying a pint of beer. *The Amato, Chalk Lane, Epsom, Surrey KT18 7AS Tel: 01372 721085*

Ewell

Map 4 ref H3

2 miles N of Epsom on the A240

It comes as something of a surprise to find shades of Xanadu in this leafy town lying just north of Epsom. ***Nonsuch Park*** is a reminder of a grand plan that Henry VIII had to build the finest palace in Christendom. Nonsuch Palace was never finished, and its only remnants have long since vanished. All that remains is the fine park that was to surround the palace, noble in stature and perspective but singularly lacking its intended focal point.

A few other historical attractions make Ewell worth visiting. There is an ancient spring which was discovered in the 17th century. The 18th century Watch House, on Church Street, was once the village lock-up. It is shaped like a small cube, with two narrow doorways under an arch. Its mean and spartan appearance alone must have deterred would-be felons.

Ewell Castle, despite its name, is not a medieval fortification. It was completed in 1814 in what was known as the Gothic style. Crenellated and stuccoed, it gives the appearance of a real castle, but the effect is somewhat lessened by its location so close to the road.

Banstead

Map 4 ref H4

3 miles E of Epsom on the A217

Banstead is one of the many small towns of Surrey that alert travellers from London that they are entering the real countryside. With the expansion of the Southeast, particularly since the last war, new suburbs have emerged and even towns that were themselves once suburbs have created their own ring of smaller satellites.

Banstead is one of the exceptions to this creeping urbanisation, and the Green Belt Act of 1938 has helped it retain much of its original country feel. It stands at the edge of the rolling green downs that provide ideal riding country. The high street has its share of nationally known outlets, but there is still a sense of local flavour and pride in its locally run firms.

All Saints Church is a small, flint and stone parish church which was built in the late 12th century and early 13th century. It has a squat appearance, with a low, broad tower and a shingled spire. Like many Surrey churches it was renovated in the 19th century. In this case the Victorian intervention was restrained, and the church now looks much as it must have in the late Middle Ages. Just north of the church is the circular ***Well***, with its large roof. The Well had formed something of a focal point in medieval times.

The Downs near Banstead are ideal for rambling. Traces of late Stone Age huts were found on the Downs and the Galley Hills are formed by four bowl barrows from that same period.

One of the most well-established businesses along Banstead High Street, ***The Woolpack*** pub is in fact the third incarnation of this pub. Comfortable tables dot the patio facing the parking area, and inside there is a sense of airiness and comfort, with knots of people tucking into the fresh food. The Woolpack is the sort of pub that

The Woolpack

doesn't scorn its roots, and you can still get a good pint of mild here. It also has a tradition of being a depot for local news, and during Victorian times parish business for the 'Town end' of the parish was transacted within its walls. The first Victorian structure was rebuilt in 1929, but lasted only 15 years, because it took a direct hit from a Nazi 'doodle bug' on 8 August 1944. The Woolpack's present manager, Gillian Sheil, is able to shed more light on this shattering event as well as the pub's general history as the village nerve centre. *The Woolpack, High Street, Banstead, Surrey SM7 2NZ Tel: 01737 354560*

Walton on the Hill *Map 4 ref H5*

5 miles S of Epsom off the A217

The *"Hill"* referred to in the name of this village is one of the many rolling hills that comprise the North Downs. Travellers heading south from London have a real sense of space by the time they reach Walton, and the upland farms strengthen this impression. Buildings - both residential and commercial - have the harmonious red-brick look so typical of this part of Surrey. They were built mainly in the Victorian era, but some of the earlier buildings were constructed from flint, hanging tile and weatherboarding.

Walton Manor is a good example of the tile-hung style and it was built in the 1890s. Its appearance shows the influence of the decorative Arts and Crafts movement, typified by architects such as Norman Shaw. Embedded in one end, however, are the walls of a stone-built manor house of the 14th century; a two storey hall and chapel protrude from the east of the house.

The view south from the centre takes in the extent of the Downs, with the North Downs Way - the traditional Pilgrim's Way to Canterbury - running along the ridge on the other side of the broad valley. In the foreground are the rolling grounds of the championship golf course.

It's hard to avoid golfing puns when you stop at ***The First Tee***, a traditional tea shop located in the heart of Walton on the Hill. The

The First Tee

menu plays the role to the hilt, hooking and slicing its way through 'the Clubhouse', 'The Bunker' and 'The Fairway' - variations on all-day breakfasts, snacks and light lunches - before settling on 'The Tee' itself, which is a choice of sandwiches, tea cakes or a traditional cream tea. Owner Sioban Lister is a welcoming presence, ably assisted by her charming young daughter. The interior is tastefully furnished, and teas are presented in attractive Royal Albert china. Sioban's husband is the keen golfer in the family, although if the cartoons dotted around the menu are anything to go by, he either has a healthy sense of humour or has gone some time since he lasted carded a sub-par round. *The First Tee, 15b Walton Street, Walton on the Hill, Surrey KT20 7RW Tel: 01737 814050*

Chipstead

Map 4 ref I5

7 miles E of Epsom on the A23

A mixture of architectural styles give Chipstead an unusual appearance, as it constitutes a mixture of Victorian model village combined with a few older houses and a good measure of suburban development. Some handsome cottages border a crossroads and there is a pretty ornamental pond in the centre. For a taste of real Victoriana, though it is worth making a short detour about half a mile south to view Shabden, a mansion built in the French Renaissance style but with a large timber porch added. The overall effect is a jarring mixture of styles that contrives to make an unattractive house out of potentially attractive ideas.

Sedilia, Coulsdon Church

Coulsdon *Map 4 ref I4*

7 miles E of Epsom on the A23

Coulsdon is a pretty village that has managed to keep recent housing developments - notably Coulsdon Woods - discreetly removed from the traditional centre. There are pretty cottages in the heart of the village and some of the more substantial farmhouses nearby can be traced to the 15th century. ***St John the Evangelist Church***, on the corner of the village green, was built in the late 13th century. The tower and spire were built more than 200 years later but the interior has some well-preserved elements from the original church. Most notable of these is the sedilla, with its circular piers and pointed arches. A sedilla was a seat for (usually three) priests and always located on the south side of the chancel.

The countryside around Coulsdon has more than its share of history. Traces of a 2nd century AD Romano-British settlement have been found on the ridge along Farthing Down, and 14 barrows on the ridge are the evidence of a 6th century Saxon burial ground. A number if iron knives, swords and other weapons have been dug from the site. ***Coulsdon Common***, on the way to Caterham, is a tranquil and largely undeveloped spot. Since Saxon times it has been common land given over to grazing, its soil deemed too poor for cultivation.

The Downlands Circular Walk conveniently begins and ends at ***The Fox***, an attractive pub facing Coulsdon Common. The present building, with benches set in the large tree-lined garden, is Victorian but there are records of a Fox ale house on this site dating back to 1720. Its pedigree as a popular local is secure, and the array of agricultural implements hanging on the walls recall the time when

The Fox

thirsty farm labourers would pause for a refreshing pint or two. Until mechanisation changed the face of farming the Fox housed the anvil and bellows of the old forge, and prints, pictures and other artefacts tell the story of how the pub was integral to the parish of Coulsdon. Three log fires and a selection of hand-pulled cask-conditioned ales add to this sense of timelessness. The Landlord can add more about the pub's history and the choice of walks in the area. He also oversees the selection of food which can be ordered from the bar, with choices covering a range of lighter lunches as well as heartier fare. *The Fox, Coulsdon Common, Caterham, Surrey CR3 5QS Tel: 01883 330401*

Chaldon

Map 4 ref I5

8 miles E of Epsom off the A23

It is well worth making the detour to Chaldon, two and a half miles to the west of Caterham, to have a look at the 11th century church of ***St Peter and St Paul*** which stands within striking distance of the old Pilgrim's Way. Although the exterior of this unassuming flint-built structure has little to commend it (other than, perhaps, its south tower and shingled spire), the interior contains one of the most outstanding medieval wall paintings still in existence in Britain. Executed in creamy white on a deep red-ochre background, the mural covers the entire west wall of the church. It is believed to have been painted around 1200, but was covered over during the Reformation and remained undiscovered until 1870. The *"Chaldon Doom"*, as it has become known, depicts gory scenes from the Last Judgement; a *"Ladder of Salvation"* can be seen reaching up to the Kingdom of Heaven from purgatory, a place where horrific punishments are meted out by fork-wielding devils to those guilty of having committed the Seven Deadly Sins. Realistic looking cauldrons, manned by infernal kitchen staff, await the wicked.

Caterham

Map 4 ref J5

8 miles E of Epsom on the B2031

The sense of being high on the North Downs is pronounced in Caterham, which lies just north of the M25. The route into the town centre from the south passes close to Foster Down, a section of the North Downs Way which incorporates the impressive ***Tupwood Viewpoint***; good views can also be enjoyed from the nearby 778 foot ***Gravelly Hill***.

Caterham itself is a modern and prosperous residential town which at first glance seems to have little to offer the casual visitor. On the other hand, the town is something of a time capsule. Until

1856 Caterham was a remote Downs village. The arrival of the railway in that year changed everything and the town developed around the new arrival and the barracks which were built in the 1870's. The railway was never extended, so Caterham is a terminus rather than a through station. As such, the 19th century town plan remains unchanged. Worthy of note, however, is the ***East Surrey Museum*** in Stafford Road which offers an interesting insight into the natural history and archaeology of the surrounding area.

Warlingham

Map 4 ref J4

8 miles E of Epsom on the B269

Successful enforcement of Green Belt policy since the Second World War has helped Warlingham retain much of its green and leafy look, and it is hard to imagine that it lies just a few miles south of bustling Croydon and its built-up suburbs. Warlingham's real fame stems from its church, ***All Saints***, or more specifically two historic events that took place in it. The new English prayer-book, authorised by Edward VI, was first used in the parish church. Its compiler, Archbishop Cranmer, attended the service. Four centuries later Warlingham parish church was chosen to host Britain's first televised church service. The church itself was restored and enlarged in Victorian times but dates from the 13th century. It still contains many old elements, including a 15th century wall painting of Saint Christopher and a 15th century octagonal font.

Modern housing has replaced most of the traditional cottages in the heart of Warlingham but there are a few survivors from past centuries. The Atwood Almshouses, a two-storey cottage flanked by single-storey cottages, were built in 1663. The vicarage, nearby, was built in the same year.

There is a distinctly equestrian feeling about ***The Harrow***, a warm and welcoming pub that is set on a quiet road on the outskirts of Warlingham. The walls, a handsome mixture of original stone and mellow panelling, are decorated with brasses, saddles, bridles and other hard evidence of horses. This theme is no affectation, because the Harrow had been the farm workers' choice of local since it was established in 1790; more recently it has attracted many customers from the several riding schools nearby. The landlady has presided over the Harrow since 1995 and is obviously a good employer because the staff match her enthusiasm and commitment. The Harrow attracts an interesting mix of local business people, ramblers and cyclists, and a good number of housewives at lunchtime. On a cold day visitors can sit by the roaring log fires and read

The Harrow

one of the newspapers or magazines provided by the pub or sample the excellent food, which includes a number of "quick refreshment" choices as well as full meals. The Harrow stocks real ales and has an impressive wine list. Meals can be taken to the large garden, which has lovely views of the adjacent common land. *The Harrow, Farleigh Road, Upper Warlingham, Surrey CR6 9EL Tel: 01883 629031*

Tatsfield *Map 4 ref J4*

10 miles E of Epsom off the B269

Tatsfield, snuggled high up on the Downs, is something of a curiosity as well as a testament to the enduring power of hyperbole in advertising. In the 1920s a group of small, unassuming cottages sprang up in the wooded landscape just north of the old village green. The verdant setting, combined with the hilly location, led to a promotional campaign urging prospective house buyer to *"Come to London Alps"*.

South of the green is ***St Mary***, the parish church which dates from about 1300. It stands on its own, commanding a fine location for panoramic views south over the Weald.

CHAPTER TWO
North Surrey

Foxwarren Park, Cobham

Chapter 2 - Area Covered

For precise location of places please refer to the colour maps found at the rear of the book.

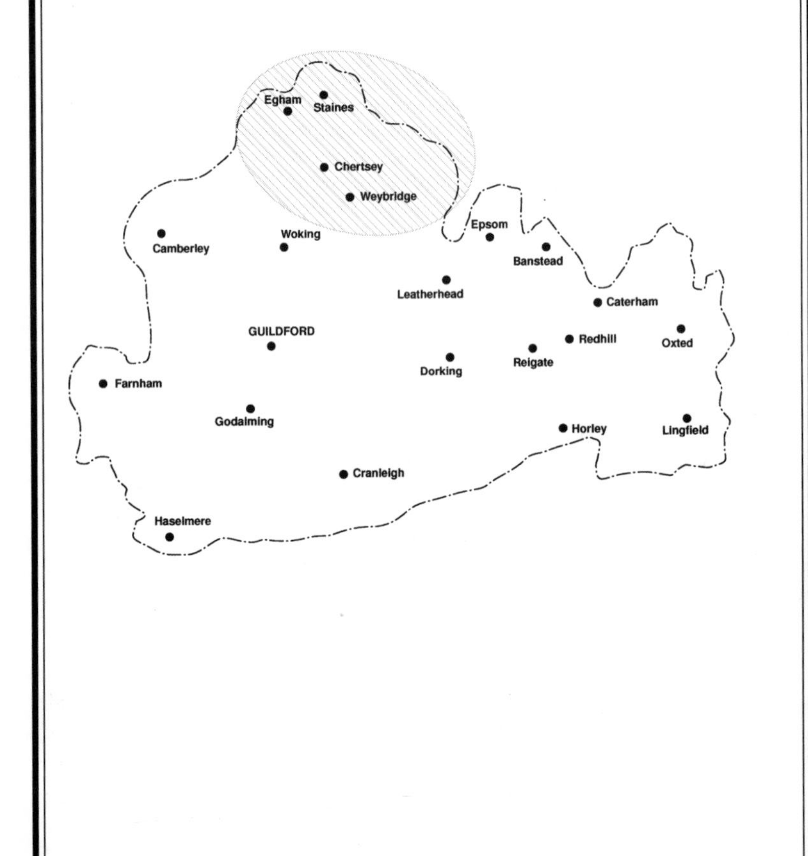

2
North Surrey

Introduction

The Thames winds through Surrey to the north of Weybridge and many of the present-day villages and towns developed as riverside trading centres in the medieval period or earlier. Romans marched through this part of Surrey during their conquest of Britain, possibly following the trail of the Celts who were already ensconced there. Saxons left their mark later, bequeathing a number of place names which duly entered the Domesday Book in the 11th century. The most impressive of all buildings along this - and perhaps any - stretch of the Thames is Hampton Court. Here England's most larger than life monarch acquired and substantially expanded Cardinal Wolsey's palace until it was fit to match his own personality.

The human mark is much in evidence on this landscape, and for every area of suburban sprawl there also seems to be a corresponding architectural gem. It might be a sensitively preserved church, as in Thorpe, or an unlikely high street survivor such as the Salvation Army Youth Centre in Sunbury-on-Thames, the newest incarnation of an impressive mansion.

Just as the Thames led to the development of medieval and earlier villages, so too did the arrival of the railway in the mid-19th century. New villages sprang up, while others expanded out of all recognition. This century's contribution to the regional transport theme is the M25, which makes a convenient western and southern border for the area covered in this chapter.

Relatively compact, yet full of interesting detail and constant surprises, this north-central section of the county is a microcosm of Surrey itself.

Weybridge

Although in many people's minds the epitome of a comfortable and modern commuter belt settlement, Weybridge is a surprisingly long-established settlement. The town takes its name from the bridge over the River Wey on the highway to Chertsey, and there is evidence of such a bridge existing as early as 1235. Tradition also links Weybridge with Julius Caesar, and many historians believe he crossed the Thames near here in 55 BC.

The town once possessed a palace, Oatlands Park, in which Henry VIII married his fifth wife, Catherine Howard, in 1540; 110 years later, the building was demolished and the stone used in the construction of the ***Wey Navigation***. Weybridge stands at the northern end of this historic inland waterway which was one of the first examples of its kind when it was completed in 1670. It extends for almost twenty miles southwards to Godalming and incorporates large sections of the main river.

The middle of the 17th century, during the Interregnum, also saw a remarkable development in Weybridge. The Diggers, a radical left-wing group, attempted to build a commune on St George's Hill, although they were thwarted by angry commoners.

Elmbridge Museum, situated in the library in Church Street, is an excellent source of information about the history - and prehistory - of Weybridge. A wide range of exhibits takes in archaeological artefacts, old maps, photographs and paintings of the district. The costume collection is particularly interesting, as it consists of clothes worn by local residents from the late 18th century to the present day.

In 1907, the worlds first purpose-built motor racing track was constructed on the Brooklands estate, near Weybridge, and in the years which followed, this legendary banked circuit hosted competitions between some of the most formidable racing cars ever made. With the outbreak of World War I, however, racing came to an end; the track fell into disrepair and Brooklands was never again able to regain its once-pre-eminent position in British motor racing.

For years, the only thing to interrupt the tranquillity of the empty track was the occasional eerie sound of screeching tyres and roaring engines, or the appearance of the goggled ghost of Percy Lambert, who tragically died after his car smashed into the end of the Railway Straight in 1913.

In recent years, the circuit has undergone something of a revival with the opening of the ***Brooklands Museum***, a fascinating establishment centred on the old Edwardian clubhouse which features a unique collection of historic racing cars, motorcycles and aircraft.

North of Weybridge

Staines *Map 1 ref E2*

6 miles N of Weybridge on the A30

The ancient town of Staines stands at the point where the old Roman road from London to the South West crossed the Rivers Thames and Colne, and in the 17th and 18th centuries, it became an important staging point on the old coaching routes to the West Country. When walking beside the Thames, look out for the London Stone which was erected in 1285 to mark the boundary of the city's authority over the river. The old part of Staines contains some noteworthy buildings, including the part 17th century church of St Mary and the town hall built in Flemish-style on the Market Place.

The Spelthorne Museum, located in the old fire station of Staines, tells the story of Staines and its extensive history. Archaeological excavations in 1969 confirmed that Staines stood on the site of the Roman settlement of Pontes. The museum contains artefacts and re-creations of life in Roman times, and provides a useful chronology for the successive riverside settlements on this site.

The M25 to the south of Staines passes close to ***Great Thorpe Park***, a 500 acre leisure park which has been built on an area of reclaimed gravel pits. The park incorporates a shire-horse centre, a series of historic reconstructions of life in ancient Britain, and a permanent theme park containing some of the latest roller coaster rides and fairground attractions.

Laleham *Map 1 ref E2*

5 miles N of Weybridge on the B376

Located only a few miles south of bustling Staines and only minutes north of the M3, Laleham might seem an unlikely candidate for "hidden gem" status. Yet it has a wonderful trump card in its setting right on the banks of the Thames, with one of London's larger reservoirs backing onto it. Water understandably plays a large part in activities here, with boat hire available just a few hundred yards west of the trim Victorian centre.

A triangular green lies near the river, reached by Ferry Lane. Facing the green are a pair of early 18th century houses, ***Muncaster House*** and ***The Coverts***.

Colourful window boxes and hanging baskets festoon the entrance of The Turks Head, a popular free house in the centre of Laleham which lies just north of Shepperton on the River Thames. Manager Viv Bennett is proud of the pub's history, which she can recount since it was built about 150 years ago. At one point in the last century it was leased to a local brewer for the staggering rent of £21 per annum. Viv is also concerned with the present, and to keep customers satisfied she stocks a wide range of real ales, beers, lagers

The Turks Head

and wines. Just as tempting is the choice of food, which is often prepared with locally produced ingredients. Light alternatives such as sandwiches, ploughman's lunches and stuffed jacket potatoes are offset by more than a dozen main meals, including daily specials. Among the favourites are the "lunchtime breakfasts", providing the ideal chance to have a hearty fry up for the first - or second - time of the day. *The Turks Head, The Broadway, Laleham, Middlesex TW18 15B, Tel: 01784 469078*

Littleton

Map 1 ref E2

5 miles N of Weybridge on the B376

Littleton has undergone a number of dramatic changes in the last four decades and today it is hard to find much of the original village lying south of the huge reservoir serving the capital. New houses, car parks and a school have replaced what had been a harmonious medieval ensemble of church, rectory, manor farm and manor house.

St Mary Magdalene

Luckily, of this group the church remains intact. ***St Mary Magdalene*** is built of brick and dates back to the 13th century. The brick is a 16th century addition, the original nave and chancel had been made of ragstone and flint rubble. This modification, which constituted a decided visual improvement, indicates a sensitivity to preservation that would be worth bearing in mind today. The west tower was built at this later date; like the earlier modifications it is of brick, giving the church a cohesive appearance. Inside there are a number of curiosities, including a late medieval locker and a complete restored set of pews from that same period. The ornate choir stalls are said to have come from Winchester.

Along the Thames

Thorpe

Map 1 ref E2

6 miles NW of Weybridge off the M25

Many of the streets in Thorpe are walled, screening residential buildings and small parks, and planning authorities succeeded in preserving this feature - unique in Surrey - despite a postwar building boom. There are some ancient elements in ***St Mary Church***, including a plain 12th century chancel arch. An 18th century monument to Elizabeth Townsend features a praying cherub. On closer inspection this cherub has an unusual, almost Mongol appearance - an effect that was something of a trademark of its designer, Sir Robert

Taylor. Old brick cottages line Church Approach. Some of the larger buildings in Littleton betray its farming background. ***Spelthorne St Mary***, on Coldharbour Lane, is a solid 18th century residence with a half-timbered barn dating from a century earlier. ***The Village Hall***, to the east of Church Approach, was converted from a 17th century brick barn.

Chertsey — *Map 1 ref E3*

3 miles NW of Weybridge on the A320

Chertsey is an ancient riverside town which has altered almost beyond recognition over the centuries. The town once boasted a formidable abbey whose influence stretched over a wide area of southern England; when it was demolished following the Dissolution of the Monasteries, its stone was used to build Hampton Court Palace and later, the River Wey Canal.

One of the abbey bells now hangs in the parish church, ***St Peter***; at one time it was used to sound the evening curfew and it is associated with a local romantic legend concerning Blanche Heriot, a young Chertsey woman who, on hearing that her lover was to be executed at the sound of the curfew bell, climbed into the tower and clung onto the tongue until his pardon arrived. This heroic action was commemorated in the ballad *"The Curfew Must Not Ring Tonight"* by the American poet Rose Hartwick Thorpe.

Despite the upheavals that Chertsey has undergone, it still manages to preserve some lovely woodland scenery, with a number of green fields and commons including ***Chertsey Mead***. A well-proportioned, seven arched bridge spans the Thames in the centre of the town.

Shepperton — *Map 1 ref F3*

3 miles N of Weybridge on the B376

Over the centuries Shepperton has capitalised on its strategic riverside location, and today's thriving market town is testimony to the entrepreneurial spirit of previous generations. It grew from its origins as a straggling collection of homesteads to become a bustling way station for west-bound traffic from London. This status was firmly established by the 15th century, and many of the lovely houses around Church Square date from that period, or shortly afterwards.

Tucked just off one end of Shepperton High Street is ***The Three Horseshoes***, an old-fashioned pub that admirably fulfils its aim to be a popular local. The comfortable interior provides a good setting for sampling some of the reasonably priced pub food, including daily

The Three Horseshoes

specials and a tempting array of toasted sandwiches. Despite the horsey theme of its title, the Three Horseshoes was once used as a sheep station, and owner Peter Cross - a New Zealander - is well placed to provide information about this aspect of the pub's history. Peter can also inform customers about the wealth of things to do in and around Shepperton. These can range from tracing cinema history in relation to the famous studio to strolling along the banks of the Thames, or even using Shepperton as a base for visits to London. Tables outside allow customers to soak up the sun or simply to linger through a long summer evening. *The Three Horseshoes, 1311 High Street, Shepperton, Middlesex TW17 9BL Tel: 01932 225726*

This century brought a new wave of development, as the famous ***Shepperton Film Studios*** were built in the 1930s. Handy for London Airport - present-day Heathrow is only a few miles to the north - as well as the capital, Shepperton presented itself as an ideal site for a film venture. International stars were collected from their transatlantic flights or from their Mayfair flats. Moreover, Shepperton's position at the edge of the Green Belt meant that "rural" locations shots could be managed just a few miles from the studios themselves.

The cosy surroundings of ***The Anchor Hotel***, set in Shepperton's quaint Church Square, don't seem to give any indication as to why this hotel would bill itself as the *"Guest residence of the rich, famous and downright dastardly"* for over 400 years. The rich and famous bit is easy enough to understand, since Lord Nelson, Charles Dickens, Elizabeth Taylor and Richard Burton must all have appreciated the discreet service and quiet comfort of the Anchor, even if some of them stayed before the arrival of colour television, en suite bathrooms and telephones in each room. The "dastardly" sting in the tail must surely refer to Dick Turpin, because the Anchor Hotel was one of his regular haunts. This might also explain the discovery of a pistol hidden in the rafters; it bore the unsettling inscription "Dick's Friend".

The Anchor Hotel

You're unlikely to find any such surprises in any of the 29 comfortable rooms, or in the traditional hotel bar which provides an ideal setting for an aperitif before trying the Anchor's excellent first-rate food. *The Anchor Hotel, Church Square, Shepperton, Middlesex TW17 9JZ Tel: 01932 221618*

The Kings Head is a handsome fifteenth century coaching inn located just off Church Square in the centre of Shepperton. It was reputedly once visited by Charles I and Nell Gwynne on their way to Windsor. More recently it became the "local" for Elizabeth Taylor and Richard Burton when they were filming at the famous Shepperton Studios. In fact, the film world still supplies the Kings Head with more than its share of regulars. David and Debs Longhurst are the popular owners and have attracted a loyal clien-

The Kings Head

tele that appreciates the fine selection of cask ales and the good food served in the bistro-style dining area that overlooks the garden. The interior has everything you would want from an old coaching inn, including low oak-beamed ceilings, a large inglenook fireplace and natural timber or stone floors. Fresh flowers - both inside and out - add a colourful touch that goes well with the mellow glow of tradition. *The Kings Head, Church Square, Shepperton TW17 9JY Tel: 01923 221910*

Walton-on-Thames

Map 1 ref F3

2 miles NE of Weybridge on the A244

Standing almost directly opposite Shepperton on the other side of the Thames is Walton-on-Thames. This unassuming London suburb has a surprisingly long and varied pedigree. As with many of the riverside communities along this stretch of the Thames, Walton has a claim to be the site where Julius Caesar forded the Thames during his second invasion of Britain. Hard archaeological evidence for this claim is scant, but there is ample proof that there was a settlement here during the Saxon period. Walton appears as "Waletona" in the Domesday Book when it was recorded as having a church, a fishery and two mills.

In 1516 Henry VIII granted the residents two fairs a year, and these continued until 1878. Walton's relations with Henry were ambivalent. However, in 1538, Walton along with surrounding communities, became incorporated with Henry VIII's Chase of Hampton Court, into what amounted to a private royal hunting preserve. Walton was outside the perimeter fence but it was forced to comply with forest law, which had a detrimental effect on cultivation. Luckily for the residents of Walton, this arrangement was discontinued when Henry died.

Until 1750 the Thames could only be crossed by ferry or ford, but in that year the first bridge was built. This original structure, a wooden toll bridge built by Samuel Dicker, was replaced by several other bridges until the present iron bridge one was built in 1864.

The part-Norman church of St Mary stands on the highest point of the town. It contains a remarkable memorial to Richard Boyle, the Viscount Shannon, which was sculpted by Louis Roubiliac in the mid 18th century.

In Manor Road is the handsome and imposing ***Manor House*** of Walton Leigh, a timber-framed brick building that dates from the Medieval period. Old records indicate that John Bradshaw, President of the Court that sentenced Charles I to death, lodged here.

Sunbury-on-Thames *Map 1 ref F2*

3 miles N of Weybridge off the M3

With its high-rise office blocks and modern shopping precincts, today's Sunbury-on-Thames seems a far cry from its earlier incarnation as market town for a riverside district that stretches from Chertsey all the way to Kingston. Yet these bastions of commerce have simply kept in step with the passing of time, and the local inhabitants seem happy enough to have retained the town's trading essence, even if it does mean that many of the period buildings have long since been replaced.

A few of the town's period buildings remain, including the ***Salvation Army Youth Centre***, which had been Sunbury Court, an 18th century mansion with Ionic decoration. Between here and St Mary Church are some handsome Georgian residences.

Robbie's and Rosie's, a popular pub in the centre of Sunbury on Thames, is proof that you don't need to have a thatched roof, sawdust, shove ha'penny or a resident ghost to meet the needs of a good local pub. Its decoration is unabashedly modern and its location is urban - right in the centre of one of Sunbury's busiest shopping arcades. The secrets to the success of Robbie's and Rosie's are many, but most relate to the couple mentioned in the pub's title. They are friendly and welcoming, as eager to make newcomers feel

Robbie's and Rosie's Bar

at home as they are to live up to their local reputation. Much of that reputation rests on the wide range of reasonably provided food and snacks, which attract a flow of local office workers each lunchtime. These are matched by an equally tempting choice of ales, beers and wines, served in the bright interior where fresh flowers adorn the tables and even the bar itself. *Robbie's and Rosie's, Sunbury Cross Centre, Sunbury Cross, Sunbury on Thames TW16 7AZ Tel: 01932 766183*

East & West Molesey — *Map 1 ref F2*

3 miles NE of Weybridge on the B369

Molesey can trace its history to the 7th century, when grants of land were made to Chertsey Abbey. Among the abbeys estates was "Muleseg", which meant Mul's field or meadow. The identity of Mul is lost in the mists of time, but his name is commemorated in two riverside communities.

The prefixes east and west, relating to Molesey, were not used until the beginning of the 13th century. In the Domesday Survey Molesey was recorded as comprising three manors tenanted by knights who had arrived with William the Conqueror. ***East Molesey*** was originally part of the parish of Kingston upon Thames but its growing independence led to its separation from Kingston under a Special Act in 1769.

East Molesey's location just opposite Hampton Court Palace provided a valuable source of income for residents, and ferries did good business until the first bridge spanned the Thames in 1753. The Bell Inn, one of the loveliest inns in Surrey, dates from the 16th century, right at the beginning of Molesey's links with Hampton Court. ***Matham Manor***, about four centuries old, is another link with the past. ***The Old Manor House***, although handsome and impressive, is something of a misnomer. It originally served as the parish workhouse and was never a manor.

Not far over the bridge from Hampton Court Palace is the ***Antiques Arcade***, the sort of emporium that Cardinal Wolsey or Henry VIII might have frequented had it been around when the Palace needed decorating. The Arcade is really a series of high quality antiques stalls, grouped together to make it easier to examine a wide range of items. It's something of an Aladdin's Cave, with good selections of jewellery, paintings, porcelain and furniture. Longcase clocks and traditional barometers line many of the walls. Although a couple of hours could pass by unnoticed in idle browsing, it is worth asking the knowledgeable stallholders about their goods - sometimes the story behind a cameo or music-holder is enough in itself to justify a purchase. As well as some ornate Victorian - and older - items, the Arcade usually has a good selection of more recent vintage, including some fine Art Deco representatives. *The Antiques Arcade, 75-77 Bridge Road, East Molesey, Surrey KT8 9HH Tel: 0181 979 7954*

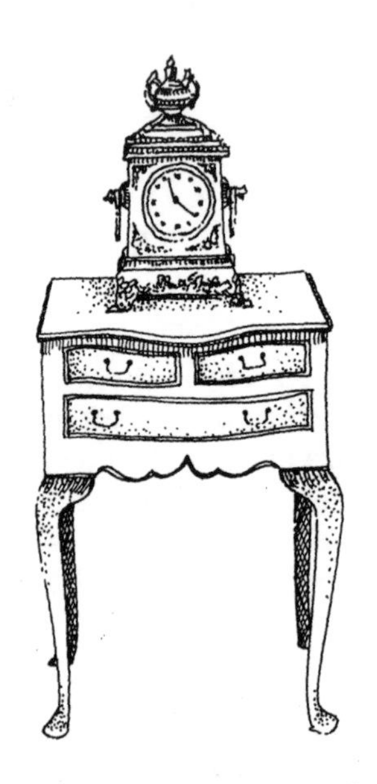

The Antiques Arcade

It is definitely best to have a close look at the exterior of ***The Bell***, one of East Molesey's most historic pubs, before entering it. If you wait until you leave, you might be inclined to dismiss what you see as the result of a libation taken inside. The Bell is known to locals as *"The Crooked House"*, and the name seems an understatement to describe the gnarled look of the pub, which seems to contain no right angles. The Bell, built in the mid-fifteenth century, has had more than five centuries to settle into its present topsy-turvy appearance. Landlords John and Denise Duff-Cole tend the

The Bell

pub with a loving care, and are eager to discuss some of its more famous customers such as Claude Duval, the dandy highwayman. But there's more to the Bell than crooked beams and history: the wide choice of mouth-watering food ensures a flow of repeat customers and the beer garden provides a chance to assess the "lines" of the pub from a different angle. *The Bell, Bell Road, East Molesey, Surrey KT8 0SS Tel: 0181 941 0400*

West Molesey is a continuation of East Molesey. It is much larger than its parent, but it occupies an even prettier stretch of the Thames. The parish church stands on a site where there has been a church since the 12th century. The present church is largely a legacy of the Victorian era, although the 15th century tower remains. Inside are some other artefacts from the medieval era, including the piscina. The piscina is a small basin in a wall niche by the altar and was used for cleaning sacramental vessels.

Molesey Hurst, a low, open stretch of land, lies along the Thames in the north of the parish. The land was once used for sporting activities such as archery, cricket, golf and even illicit duelling. It can also claim a cricketing "first". It was here, in 1795, that a player was first given out leg-before-wicket.

Hampton Court *Map 1 ref F2*

4 miles NE of Weybridge on the A309

The name of Henry VIII is forever linked with the magnificent palace and grounds occupying a stretch of the Thames some 13 miles southwest of London. Its stature and extensive gardens underpin its role as the most impressive of all royal residences, but Hampton Court was originally designed with a slightly different purpose in mind. It was the brainchild of Cardinal Wolsey, who had it built in 1516.

Wolsey was an ambitious and powerful man, serving as Henry VIII's Lord Chancellor, so Hampton Court was never likely to remain simply an ecclesiastical abode. Banquets and balls were the order of the day, and Hampton Court gained such fame - or notoriety - that it prompted a certain amount of envy from the monarch. In 1525 Henry asked the Cardinal why he had built such a palace for himself and Wolsey, interpreting the potentially dangerous undercurrents, replied *"to show how noble a palace a subject may offer to his sovereign"*. Even this huge gift was not enough to secure Wolsey's position. Four years later, after he had failed to secure a papal annulment for Henry's marriage to Catherine of Aragon, Wolsey found himself stripped of all his possessions, including the palace of Whitehall. He fell ill and died within a year.

Hampton Court continued to grow under the ownership of Henry, who enlarged the kitchens, altered many rooms and rebuilt the chapel. It became the home of the last five of Henry's wives as well as a growing number of courtiers and assorted royal hangers-on.

Approached through ***Trophy Gate***, Hampton Court gives a first impression of grandeur and scale. The courtyards and buildings to the left still contain a number of "grace and favour" apartments, where Crown officials and dependants of the Royal family live. Two side turrets contain terracotta roundels with the images of Roman emperors which date from Wolsey's time. Anne Boleyn's gateway, opposite Base Court, is carved with the initials H and A, for Henry and Anne.

To the left of Clock Court, with its large astronomical clock, is the ***Great Hall***, which Henry had completed in 1534, having forced the builders to work night and day. Mounted stag heads and fine tapestries line the walls beneath the intricate hammerbeam roof. The Great Hall was the scene of theatrical productions during the reigns of Elizabeth I and James I, and among the performing troupes was that of William Shakespeare. Under the Great Hall are the

The Great Hall, Hampton Court

Tudor Kitchens, with their huge fireplaces and assortment of ancient cooking utensils.

The ***Queen's Apartments*** were built for Mary II, but were only completed after her death. They are reached by the grand Queen's Staircase which leads to the Queen's Guard Chamber. Life-sized marble guardsmen flank the main chimneypiece. The Queen's state rooms run along the east wing of Fountain Court, and include the Queen's Drawing Room and the Queen's Bedroom. The Queen's Gallery contains ornate marble fireplaces with mantelpieces decorated with images of doves and Venus. Gobelins tapestries, on the theme of Alexander the Great, hang from the walls.

The King's Staircase also features Alexander the Great, although in this case it is really William III in the role of Alexander. The staircase leads to the ***King's Apartments***, which comprise William's state rooms. A display of arms, numbering 3,000 pieces, is arranged in the King's Guard Chamber, set out as they would have been during William's time.

Outside are the ***Palace Gardens***, Hampton Court's main attraction for many visitors and reflecting the influence of three kings: Henry VIII, Charles II and William III. William, with his Dutch background, was perhaps the most involved of these monarchs, and his influence is particularly evident in the Fountain Garden, fanning out from the east front and now mostly lawn, and the Privy Garden to the south of the Palace. The Privy Garden is being restored: shrubberies that were allowed to grow there in the 19th century have been removed to reveal traces of the formal beds and pathways that were William's legacy. A fully re-created 17th century formal garden will be the result of this horticultural archaeology.

The ***Broad Walk*** runs from the Thames for half a mile past the east front and is lined with herbaceous borders. Just off the walk to the left and inside is the Tudor Tennis Court, a Real Tennis court built by Henry VIII, who was a keen player. To the north of the Palace is the famous ***Maze***, planted in 1714 within William III's "Wilderness" of evergreen trees. The Maze is extremely popular and can be surprisingly difficult to negotiate. Be warned.

Thames Ditton — *Map 1 ref G3*

3 miles E of Weybridge on the A309

Thames Ditton is one of the two Dittons that lie along the Thames south of Hampton Court. The name probably derives from the "dictun", or farm by the dyke, and there were already a Saxon church and five manors in the area at the time of the Domesday Book. The heart of Thames Ditton dates mainly from the 19th century, but the harmonious blend of red brick and occasional black-timbered buildings along the High Street help put visitors in mind of the earlier history.

A flower-decked path leads to ***St Nicholas' Church***, which was first mentioned in the 12th century - roughly the time when Ditton was divided into two parishes. The building is of flint and stone and the interior contains a font decorated with mysterious motifs that still puzzle historians. Thames Ditton benefited from its proximity to Hampton Court Palace and the church contains the grave of Cuthnert Blakeden, "Serjeant of the confectionary to King Henry the Eighth".

Ye Olde Harrow is a good-sized and well-proportioned pub and restaurant on the attractive outskirts of Thames Ditton. The visitor's first impressions - for most customers this is when they leave their cars in the spacious car park - are of the stunning displays of hanging baskets and overflowing tubs of flowers that line the front of the pub. The horticultural theme continues, albeit in a slightly different key, inside where chef-proprietor Adrian Curtin calls on the freshest local produce to create an admirable range of home-cooked food. The sense of size and space, hinted at from the outside, are confirmed although there is no feeling of being lost in some cav-

Ye Olde Harrow

ernous interior. Instead, Ye Olde Harrow provides that happy balance of plentiful table and bar space coupled with quiet corners for a cosy drink or a chance to contemplate the papers in peace. Picnic tables outside enjoy views of Weston Green Road, offering the visitor the chance to imagine life at Ye Olde Harrow a couple of centuries ago when it was the haunt of highwaymen. *Ye Olde Harrow, Weston Green Road, Thames Ditton, Surrey KT7 0JZ Tel: 0181 3981688*

Long Ditton

Map 1 ref G3

4 miles E of Weybridge on the A309

There is a peculiar lack of logic in the naming of the two Dittons; Thames Ditton is actually longer than Long Ditton but this more easterly village has an longer history than its neighbour. ***St Mary's Church***, in the heart of Long Ditton, is a relative newcomer, having been built in 1880 but it stands close to the site of a Saxon church built long before the Dittons separated into two parishes.

Long Ditton is a scattered parish, with only a few vestiges left of its extensive history. Much of its history, however, can be gleaned from a close look inside St Mary's. The interior of the church features monuments to the Evelyn family, who put Long Ditton on the map in the 16th and 17th centuries. George Evelyn, grandfather of the famous diarist John Evelyn, acquired the local manor in the late 16th century and then set about establishing gunpowder mills in the area. Business for gunpowder was booming, so to speak, in this turbulent period and the Evelyns amassed a huge fortune, eventually spreading their business further afield within Surrey.

South and East of Weybridge

Oatlands — *Map 1 ref E4*

1 mile E of Weybridge on the B374

"The land where oats were grown" gave its name to the Tudor palace in Oatlands Park. This was already an established residence when Henry VIII forced its owner to cede him the title in 1538. Henry was in a rush to build a palace for his new queen, Anne of Cleves, although Ann never lived at Oatlands. However, the palace did become the home of subsequent monarchs, including Elizabeth I, James I and Charles I. In fact it was Charles who is said to have planted the proud cedar tree that stands beside the drive of what is now the ***Oatlands Park Hotel***; he was celebrating the birth of his son, Prince Henry of Oatlands.

Oatlands Village on the outskirts of Weybridge was the scene of great royal activity during the Tudor period so it should come as no surprise to find a pub bearing the name of ***The Prince of Wales***. This popular local dates from the middle of the 19th century so the sovereign in question was probably not Henry VIII who built a royal residence (now demolished) in Oatlands. The Prince of Wales occu-

The Prince of Wales

pies a sunny corner location and is very much part of the local fabric. Landlords Brian and Pat Ford take a great deal of pride in the pub, which presents a riot of blossoming colour from hanging baskets in the summer and welcomes customers with its blazing fire in colder weather. One reason for the pub's popularity is its home-prepared food, which is reasonably priced, fortifying and served with flair. *The Prince of Wales, Anderson Road, Oatlands Village, Weybridge, Surrey KT13 9NX Tel: 01932 852082*

Whiteley Village *Map 1 ref F4*

2 miles SW of Weybridge on the B365

A mile and a half to the southwest of Weybridge, and close to the St George's Hill residential area much-favoured by famous media personalities, lies the remarkable ***Whiteley Village***. This unique 200 acre model village was founded on the instructions of the proprietor of a famous Bayswater department store who in 1907, left one million pounds in his will to house his retired staff. The community was designed to be self-contained with its own churches, hospital and shops, and was laid out in an octagonal pattern around a green containing a memorial to the project's benefactor. The site has been planted with a great many trees and flowering shrubs, and is best visited in late-spring and summer.

Hersham *Map 1 ref F3*

3 miles E of Weybridge on the A307

Anglo-Saxons were the likeliest first settlers of Hersham, although prehistoric flint tools have been found on what is now Southwood Farm. In the 12th century the village was spelt Haverichesham and probably pronounced *"Haverick's Ham"*. Two major events have shaped Hersham's history. The first occurred in 1529 when Henry VIII acquired Hampton Court from Cardinal Wolsey. Henry decided that his new estate lacked one of its necessities - a deer park - so he set about buying adjacent land and encircling the area with a perimeter fence. Other villages, such as Weybridge and Esher, were on the edge of the park and escaped being enclosed, but Hersham was not so lucky. Not surprisingly, Hersham had a well-developed anti-royalist streak by the time of the Civil War and one of Cromwell's prominent aides, Captain John Inwood, lived there.

Politics and warfare apart, Hersham continued largely untouched by the outside world until the 19th century. The arrival of the railway in 1838 led to a huge rise in its population. Development accompanied this boom and much of Hersham's original appearance was altered completely. Local residents, however, would not let the process rip the heart out of their village. ***Hersham Green***, once common land, was actually enlarged in 1878. It is now used for a variety of local functions including a popular Summer Fayre with traditional entertainment.

Cobham *Map 1 ref F4*

4 miles S of Weybridge off the A3

Cobham is a busy residential town, mostly given over to densely settled residential streets. However, it does possess a pair of fine period buildings, which dominate a bend of the River Mole on the southeastern side of Cobham. Cedar House, built in the mid-18th century, is a solid and well-proportioned brick building which actually changes height halfway along its front. To the rear is a medieval section which includes a large tracery window. Built somewhat earlier in the18th century is ***Ham Manor***, with a mansard roof and an impressive Italianite decrease.

Nothing about the entrance to the ***Exchange Bar Diner*** in Cobham - with its porticoed entrance and classical symmetry - gives a clue to the fact that inside is a chance to visit the various cooking styles of America. A young, friendly staff take customers through choices ranging from Cajun and Mexican to other stateside favourites such as burgers, steaks, imaginative salads and seafood (including grilled catfish). Special offers such as the "Sundowner" (any

Exchange Bar Diner

two courses) and "Light Grazin" cater to appetites that aren't ready for the full treatment. Service is prompt and informative, in the true American style, and customers can sample a range of New World wines and American beers. Many of the belt-loosening desserts centre on Steve's Ice Cream, a legend across the Atlantic. There is another chance to sample the wide choice of the Exchange Bar Diner at its other branch in Guildford's Ladymead Retail Park. *Exchange Bar Diner, Cobham, Surrey, Tel: 01932 862015*

About a mile north of Cobham is ***Foxwarren Park***, a bizarre house with eerie gables and multi-coloured bricks. It was built in 1860, and contemporary Victorian architects were known to introduce a bit of macabre humour into some of their designs. In this case it is hard to decide whether the intended effect was self-mocking or whether the gloomy appearance conformed to the owner's tastes.

Foxwarren Park

One mile west of Cobham is ***Painshill Park***, a white 18th century house with a fine setting on a hill. The house is impressive but Painshill is more noted for its grounds, which were laid out by the Hon. Charles Hamilton, son of the Earl of Abercorn, in the 1740s. These grounds were a talking point in the mid-18th century and were praised by luminaries such as Horace Walpole. Hamilton had let his imagination conjure up a series of landscapes and ornaments that created a profoundly Romantic atmosphere. An ornamental lake lay in front of a Gothic brick abbey, while on an island in the lake were various tufa sculptures and perpendicular cliffs leading down to the water. Hamilton even built a hermitage, and then went one stage further by installing a hermit in it. The mounting catalogue of expenses took its toll on Hamilton, however, and he eventually went bankrupt. Most of the features in the grounds are also sadly gone.

Stoke D'Abernon

Map 1 ref F4

4 miles S of Weybridge off the A3

Like Cobham, the northern part of Stoke d'Abernon is undistinguished; however, the older southern part, which reaches down to the River Mole, contains a fine mid 18th century part-Palladian, part-baroque manor house and an exceptional parish church which is believed to be among the oldest in the country.

The south wall of ***St Mary's Church*** is believed to date back to the days of St Augustine in the 7th century, and indeed it has been found to contain brickwork and cornices belonging to a Roman structure which once stood on the site. There are also traces of an early Saxon lord's gallery and one of the oldest monumental brasses in Britain, that of Sir John d'Abernon who was buried in 1277. The church, with its wonderful mixture of styles and influences, is certainly worth a look; the north aisle is 12th century, the rib-vaulted chancel 13th century, the stained-glass part-medieval, and the magnificent walnut pulpit early 17th century.

About half a mile south of Stoke d'Abernon is ***Slyfield Manor***, which was built in the 17th century but incorporated a late medieval timber-frame building. Garden walls, with original archways,

Slyfield Manor

blend with the painstaking brickwork of the house to create an effect that reminds many visitors of the work of Inigo Jones, particularly in Covent Garden.

Oxshott

Map 1 ref G4

4 miles SE of Weybridge off the A3

Taking its name from the Old English for "Occa's Wood", Oxshott remained a small hamlet set in woods and heather until the 1880s, when the completion of the Surbiton to Guildford Railway ushered in an era of growth and development. Some stretches of this original woodland have withstood the tide of new roads and houses, notably ***Oxshott Heath*** and ***Princes Coverts***, which is a woodland owned by the Crown Estate. In the middle of Princes Coverts is a square red-brick building which was erected in the 18th century over a medicinal spring known as *"Jessop's Well"*. The mineral content of the spring water was said to compare with that of Cheltenham, but despite the Royal connection and the salubrious waters, Oxshott somehow never achieved true spa status.

Perhaps Oxshott was considered a bit too dissipated because for many years it was mildly notorious for having two public houses but no church. This imbalance between sacred and profane was partly offset in 1912, when St Andrew's Church was erected.

Claygate

Map 1 ref G3

4 miles SE of Weybridge off the A3

Standing on a rich geological seam where dense London clay meets Bagshot sand, Claygate is well named. For many years this rich earth provided a living for many local men, who would have to bear the brunt of jibes from neighbouring villagers about working in the Claygate "treacle mines". Taunts notwithstanding, Claygate did supply the raw material for countless bricks and fireplaces.

Claygate can trace its origins to the Saxon times when it was a manor within the parish of Thames Ditton. In the early Medieval period the estate passed into the ownership of Westminster Abbey, which retained possession until Henry VIII dissolved the monasteries. Henry simply added it to his estates in Hampton Court.

Constrained for centuries by monastic, then royal, control, Claygate remained largely unchanged as a tiny community until the 19th century. In 1838, however, Claygate Common was enclosed, enabling residents to enlarge the village considerably. One of the first orders of business was to erect their own church, Holy Trinity, to save the two-mile walk to Thames Ditton.

Ruxley Towers is an interesting building that dates from the same period. It has a Gothic tower, built in 1830 and is decorated with a frightening display of gargoyles.

Occupying a leafy corner site in the village of Claygate is ***The Swan***, an old-fashioned inn that attracts a loyal local following as well as thirsty passers-by. Claygate is one of those villages within easy striking distance of London and yet providing a window on to a

The Swan Inn

way of life that seems unchanged by mobile phones and urgent deadlines. Sitting outside at one of the tables in front offers the chance to engage in that quintessentially English activity - watching cricket being played on the village green opposite. In fact, a plaque outside the Swan announces that it is the home of the Leverets Cricket Club (befitting the address on Hare Lane). Inside, the Swan has a real Edwardian feel about it, reflecting the fact that it was rebuilt in 1902. Proprietor Tim Kitch is a popular landlord, dispensing local knowledge along with his pints. His food, including a changing array of blackboard specials, covers a wide range and ensures a steady flow of repeat customers. *The Swan Inn, 2 Hare Lane, Claygate, Surrey KT10 9BS Tel: 01372 462582*

Esher

Map 1 ref G3

4 miles S of Weybridge off the A3

The part 16th century St George's church has an unusual three-tier pulpit and a marble monument to Princess Charlotte of Wales who died at nearby Claremont House in 1817. The part of Surrey nearest to London is well supplied with racecourses: as well as at Kempton Park, near Sunbury, and at the classic course at Epsom, regular meetings are held at ***Sandown Park*** on Esher's northern edge.

Near here, and well worth a visit is the beautiful National Trust-owned ***Claremont Landscape Garden*** which lies on the southern side of the A307 Portsmouth road within a mile of the town centre. Having been laid out in the 1710s, this is believed to be one of the earliest surviving examples of an English landscape garden; later in the century, it was remodelled by William Kent whose work was continued by Capability Brown. The grounds have been designed to include a number of striking vistas and contain a grassed amphitheatre, grotto, lake, and an island with a pavilion. Nearby ***Claremont House*** operates as a school and is only occasionally open to visitors. It was designed in the 1700s by Vanbrugh and substantially remodelled in 1772 for Clive of India.

One of the architects who undertook the renovation was Lancelot, or "Capability", Brown who not only remodelled the gardens but oversaw much of the work on the building itself.

CHAPTER THREE
Northwest Surrey

Bisley Church

Chapter 3 - Area Covered

For precise location of places please refer to the colour maps found at the rear of the book.

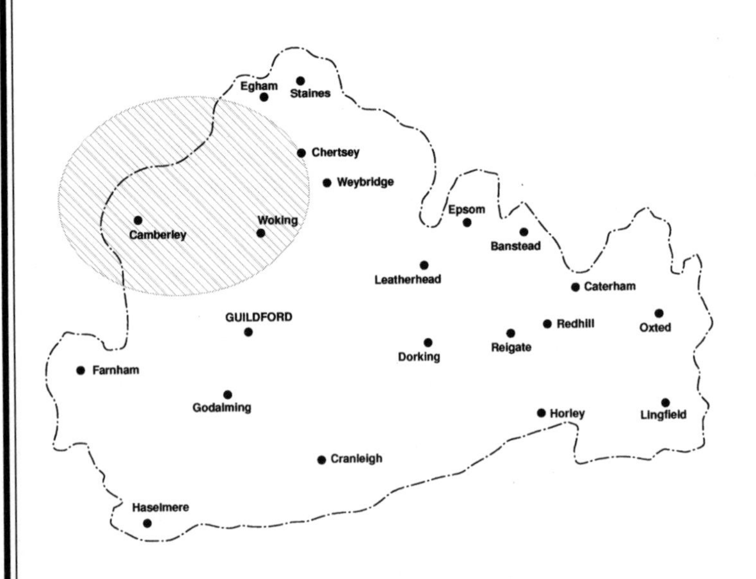

3
Northwest Surrey

Introduction

The northwest corner of Surrey, lying to the west of the M25 and stretching westwards to the Berkshire and Hampshire borders and given a southern limit by the A3, shows the county's countryside coming into its own. Rich farming areas give way to expanses of heath and dotted woodlands, once the haunt of highwaymen but now safe for ramblers - as long as they steer clear of the well-marked military areas.

Woking is the principal town in this area, like may Surrey towns an established centre that was transformed by the arrival of the railway in the 19th century. The Victorian influence is strong throughout this part of Surrey, evident in many of the larger houses built by or under the auspices of Norman Shaw and other proponents of the Arts and Crafts style which blossomed as a reaction against poor-quality, mass-produced building materials.

The more ornate style of Victorian architecture, which seems to be the embodiment of a prosperous nation flexing its imperial muscle, is also represented in the two massive buildings funded by Thomas Holloway, the Royal Holloway and Bedford New College and the Holloway Sanatorium which are near Egham in the north. That same northern extremity contains the site of one of England's defining moments, the signing of the Magna Carta in 1215 at the riverside meadow of Runnymede.

Elsewhere, and particularly along the western fringes by the Hampshire border, visitors can sense the presence of medieval monastic communities, Roman encampments and Iron Age and even earlier fortified settlements. All of these sites are easily accessible, and the routes between major attractions are peppered with attractive pubs, charming guest houses and museums telling the story of Surrey's heritage.

Woking

Woking is a commuter town which lies on the main railway line to Waterloo. In fact it was the railway that defined the present appearance - and location - of Woking. The original village was what is now called Old Woking, and when the railway arrived in 1838 the station was built 2 miles away in what was then open heathland. The town developed around this new arrival, and the original village centre dwindled as the population was drawn towards new employment. As a result, most of the heart of Woking dates from the middle of the 19th century.

Among these Victorian-era buildings, however, is an unexpected "first". The first purpose-built mosque to be founded in Britain - ***Shah Jehan Mosque*** - can be found in Woking's Oriental Street. The construction of this unusual onion-domed structure was largely financed by the ruler of the Indian state of Bhopal who visited the town in 1889.

Old Woking is a former market town which is now incorporated into the southeastern suburbs of its more modern neighbour. This is an old settlement, dating from the Saxon period and mentioned in the Domesday Book. Old Woking had the good fortune to be listed as a personal possession of the king and therefore it did not need to pay taxes. Its streets contain some noteworthy old buildings, including the 17th century old Manor House, and the part-Norman parish church of St Peter which has a late-medieval west tower.

East House, which offers traditional bed and breakfast accommodation in the quiet outskirts of Woking, holds some pleasant surprises for visitors. From the outside it resembles the other white-fronted villas on this tranquil leafy street. Inside each of the three bedrooms, however, are Russian Orthodox icons and other items giving a clue as to the origins of the owners, Doctor and Mrs Vladimir Moss. Friendly and welcoming, Mrs Moss is only too happy to regale visitors with accounts of her homeland. In keeping with her adopted country, however, she has been bitten with the gardening bug, and the results are a joy to observe. Some of the bedrooms, as well as the bow-windowed sitting room, look out on to the extensive

East House

and well-maintained garden. East House is within easy striking distance of Woking, with its fine shops, and is also handy for the A320 and Guildford. There is a choice of pubs around the corner for quick evening meals. *East House, Beech Hill, Mayford, Woking, Surrey GU22 0SB Tel: 01483 763218*

South and East from Woking

Pyrford

Map 2 ref E4

1 mile SE of Woking on the B382

Located roughly midway between Woking and Byfleet is Pyrford, which manages to retain many aspects of its village character despite being no more than a couple of miles from its larger neighbours. It is set in meadows along the River Wey, with most of its original red-brick cottages still forming a core near the church. This parish church, the largely-Norman ***Church of St Nicholas***, has been preserved over the centuries without being the victim of intrusive restoration work. The south wall of the nave contains some unusual wall paintings of the Flagellation and Christ's Passion which were painted around 1200. Research work carried out in the 1960s uncovered some even earlier murals beneath these paintings. The murals depict horsemen as well as a mysterious procession of men carrying staves.

About half a mile along the B367, to the south of Pyrford, is ***Newark Priory***, an evocative ruin set in fields along the banks of the Wey. The priory was a house of Austin Canons who founded it in the 12th century. Like other monastic settlements it was a victim of the Dissolution under Henry VIII. Unlike others, however, it was never converted into a private residence. Instead its walls were broken down for use in local buildings, although some of its features - including the east window - are said to have been taken to Ockham. Today only the walls of the south transept and those of the presbytery still stand, and visitors must use their imagination to work out where in the surrounding corn fields there might once have been the remainder of the monastic buildings.

Wisley

Map 1 ref E4

3 miles E of Woking off the A3

The Royal Horticultural Society's internationally renowned ***Wisley Garden*** lies on the north side of the A3, one mile to the northwest of Ockham. As well as containing a wide variety of trees, flowering shrubs and ornamental plants, this magnificent 250 acre garden incorporates the Society's experimental beds where scientific trials are conducted into new and existing plant varieties. Wisley also acts as a centre for training horticultural students, and offers a wide range of plants, books, gifts and gardening advice at its first-class plant centre and shop.

Church Farm House lies between the River Wey and its navigation canal, about half a mile from the RHS garden at Wisley. It is a traditional timbered red brick farm house dating from the early sixteenth century and is adjacent to Wisley church, which is four hundred years older. It has a spacious vaulted kitchen, dining and

Church Farm House

living area, a large and comfortable drawing room, and various other bits and pieces which include fax and e-mail facilities for guests who can't live without them. On the first floor are two bedrooms, one double and one small double or large single. On the second floor - the former grain store - are a large twin-bedded room and a single room. Deirdre and Christopher Geer are warm and often entertaining hosts, and there is a good range of shops and restaurants within a mile or so. *Church Farm House, Wisley, Surrey GU23 6QL Tel: 01932 351683*

Ripley — *Map 1 ref E5*

2 miles E of Woking off the A3

Just a mile or so to the southwest of Wisley is the attractive village of Ripley, a former staging post on the old coaching route between London and Portsmouth. The main street contains a number of exceptional brick and half-timbered buildings, including the charming ***Vintage Cottage*** with its unusual crownpost roof.

Most of the attractive houses lie on the gracefully curving High Street. Unusually, the long and wedge-shaped village green lies beside the street on the west side. The village seems to have grown away from the green rather than around as in most English villages.

Sutton Place — *Map 1 ref E5*

2 miles SE of Woking off the A3

Sutton Place was the creation of Sir Richard Weston, a protege of Henry VIII who was a Knight of the Bath, a Gentleman of the Privy Chamber and eventually Under-Treasurer of England. He had accompanied Henry to France for the famous meeting at the Field of the Cloth of Gold in 1520, so in every respect he had the right to expect to live in sumptuous surroundings that reflected his high standing.

The house he had built, after receiving the grant of the Sutton estate in 1521, is seen by many critics as one of the most important English houses to be built in the years after Hampton Court was completed. It was built to describe almost a perfect square, with sides measuring about 130-140 feet surrounding a central courtyard. The north side was demolished in the 18th century, so today's house appears to comprise a two-storey, red brick central building with two long projections. Symmetry is important in Sutton Place, as English architects were busy putting to use the elements of the Italian Renaissance in their buildings. Doorways and windows are balanced in each wing.

Terracotta Panels, Sutton Place

The Italian influence is particularly evident in the terracotta ornamentation of the windows and even more dramatically in a series of terracotta panels depicting cherubs over the entrance. Terracotta had been first used as an architectural feature, mainly as faience or majolica, in Hampton Court in 1521. Sutton Court was built probably no more than a decade later - records show that Henry VIII was a guest in 1533 - so it was obviously at the forefront of this style of ornamentation.

It is the exterior, with its strict adherence to Renaissance tenets, that makes Sutton Place so fascinating. Inside there have been alterations and additions that make the effect less wholly linked to one period.

Worplesdon
Map 2 ref D5

3 miles SW of Woking on the A322

Worplesdon retains a sense of its rural past in its setting on the edge of heaths, despite the threat posed by the expansion of Guildford which is just a couple of miles to the south. A number of brick houses dating from the early 18th century surround the triangular green, which is up on a hill. One of these houses displays a brick front, of around 1700, tacked on to a timber frame, creating an unusual effect.

St Mary Church stands proudly above the village. Although clumsily restored in the Victorian era, the church has a number of interesting features from the medieval period. Chief among these is the late 15th century tower, which is compact and well proportioned. At its base is a tower arch over an intricately carved door. The inner face has an inscription which reads *"Richard Exfold made XIV fote of yis touor"*.

North to Runnymede

Bisley

Map 2 ref D4

3 miles W of Woking on the A322

Surrounded by farmland and heaths, Bisley remains resolutely small-scale and unassuming. It is within easy reach of Camberley to the west and Woking to the east, but luckily much of the traffic comes in the form of ramblers who are equipped with the well-marked books of pub walks in the vicinity. Bissell's contribution to the pub supply is the Fox Inn, which stands opposite Snowdrop Farm, where a well-marked trail crosses the A322. Having crossed the A322, the trail cuts southwestwards across ***Bisley Common***, where annual marksmanship competitions are held on the rifle ranges, past the pretty little Stafford Lake and into Sheet's Heath. Even making this short walk, which in fact is part of one of the longer "pub" trails,

Bisley Church

gives a good indication of the native landscape. Here the land is more or less in its natural state, with scrubby low bushes and bracken indicating why it was the more fertile soil east of the A322 that was more sought after for cultivation.

The attractive church of ***St John the Baptist*** likewise stands to the west of most houses in Bisley, giving it an almost lonely appearance. It is built of local sandstone with a short tiled spire topping its wooden tower.

Chobham *Map 2 ref D4*

3 miles NW of Woking on the A3046

Enjoying a peaceful location just five minutes drive from Woking town centre is the attractive community of Chobham. The village High Street is an attractive and generally harmonious stretch of 18th century brick and stucco houses. The street itself curves up a hill, with the parish church of St Laurence punctuating the row about halfway along. The original church was built in the 11th century but a restructuring in 1170 was the first of many alterations that have left the church more of an assembly of disparate elements than a harmonious whole.

Virginia Water *Map 2 ref D3*

7 miles N of Woking on the A30

From Camberley, the A30 runs along the northeastern border of the county to Virginia Water, a surprising diversion which lies in the heart of the Surrey stockbroker belt. The "water" referred to is a mile and a half long artificial lake which is set within mature woodland at the southern end of ***Windsor Great Park***; it was created by Paul and Thomas Sandby, two accomplished Georgian landscapers who were also known for their painting. The picturesque ruins standing at the lakeside are genuine remains of a Roman temple which once stood at Leptis Magna in Libya. ***The Valley Gardens*** also contain an unusual 100 foot totem pole which was erected here in 1958 to mark the centenary of British Columbia. A little further to the north, the ***Savill Garden*** is renowned as one of the finest woodland gardens in the country.

The famous ***Wentworth Golf Course*** lies on the opposite side of the A30 on the southern edge of the genteel settlement which takes its name from the Sandbys' lake.

Englefield Green *Map 1 ref D2*

8 miles N of Woking on the A30

The green that gives Englefield Green its name is large and attractive, flanked by a number of pretty houses which include some that are several centuries old. Two of the finest are located at the north-eastern corner of the green. The aptly named ***Old House*** was built in 1715, and most of it is a tribute to the red brick symmetry so beloved of that Queen Anne Period. Next to it is ***Englefield House***, built about a century later. This is more of a curiosity, since it seems that the architect was unclear whether his brief called for something classical, neo-Gothic or Venetian.

Lying just a mile or two from the Thames within the village of Englefield Green is ***The Armstrong Gun***, a popular pub that attracts a loyal following of locals and visitors to the village. Built in 1870, it somehow feels even older than that, perhaps because of the low ceilings - a legacy of the pub's previous history as two cottages. Landlord Stewart Gordon is a welcoming host and plays a major role in village affairs; he is a mine of information about local fishing, cricket and walks along the Thames. Customers have a wide

The Armstrong Gun

choice of drinks as well as food, which can be eaten in the new dining room or in the good-sized garden. Englefield Green retains something of its rustic character and was the site of the last recorded fatal duel in England, between two exiled Frenchmen in 1845. Nowadays it is famous for somewhat more polite combat - as it is the host of the World Marbles Championships. *The Armstrong Gun, 49 Victoria Street, Englefield Green, Egham, Surrey TW20 0WX Tel: 01784 433000; Fax: 01784 477554*

Egham

Map 1 ref D2

8 miles N of Woking on the A30

Skirted by the River Thames and the historic fields of Runnymede, Egham has two great advantages, yet at first glance this north Surrey town seems to fall well below expectations. A closer look, however, shows that Egham contains, or at least is near, a number of points of real interest. The centre of Egham is not particularly noteworthy, standing across the river from Staines and reflecting the latter's somewhat featureless appearance. The only genuinely attractive district is the small area by the Swan Hotel at the Staines Bridge, where there is a pretty row of riverside cottages.

At Egham Hill, a couple of miles to the north, however, is one of Surrey's more memorable buildings, the ***Royal Holloway and Bedford New College***. This institution is housed in a huge Victorian building which was modelled on the Chateau du Chambord in the Loire Valley in France. It is in the form of a double quadrangle, measuring 550 feet in length and 376 feet across. Thomas Holloway, the eminent businessman and philanthropist, had it built as a college for women - male students were only admitted in 1965 - where they could study for degrees at any university. His generous ideas on lodging - each student was allocated two rooms - dictated the enormous size of the building. The college incorporates a notable gallery of 19th century paintings and a concert hall which offers regular programmes of music and drama.

Holloway Sanatorium, which lies a couple of miles southwest of the college, was built as a companion piece to it. It opened in 1887, three years before the college. Like its companion, Holloway Sanatorium looked to the Continent for inspiration; in this case it is the architecture of Bruges and Ypres that acts as a catalyst for another display of Victorian exuberance. The result is a brick and stone Gothic structure that stands - with the college - as the epitome of High Victorian fashion. Ironically, both of these buildings were constructed after that overblown style had begun to ebb. One explanation for this time lag is that the architect of the Sanatorium, W. H. Crossland, was from the North Country and was therefore less aware of - or swayed by - London fashion.

Runnymede

Map 1 ref D2

10 miles N of Woking on the A30

A meadow beside the River Thames to the north of Egham is where King John sealed the Magna Carta in 1215. The historic ***Runnymede Site*** and nearby ***Cooper's Hill*** are contained within a 300 acre tract of land which is now under the ownership of the National Trust.

The area contains three separate memorials: a domed neoclassical temple which was erected by the American Bar Association to commemorate the sealing of the world's first bill of democratic rights, a memorial to John F Kennedy, and the Air Forces Memorial which was erected in memory of the World War II airmen who went missing in action.

From the top of Cooper's Hill there are magnificent views across Windsor Great Park and the Thames Valley. The river below is populated by slow-moving motor cruisers and pleasure craft, and river trips to Windsor, Staines and Hampton Court can be taken from Runnymede, daily between May and October, and at weekends during winter. The nearby ***Runnymede Pleasure Ground*** offers a range of children's leisure activities in a pleasant riverside setting.

The Western Fringe

Windlesham *Map 2 ref C3*

7 miles W of Woking on the A30

Windlesham lies on the western edge of Surrey, on the Berkshire border. It is far prettier than its larger southern neighbour Bagshot, which Daniel Defoe described as *"not only good for little but good for nothing"*. Bagshot today bears out Defoe's description, being built up with unimaginative suburban sprawl.

Windlesham, on the other hand, retains much of its original rural aspect, lying in a setting of heath and meadow. Victorian brick buildings - including some larger examples of the "prosperous merchant" variety - line the heath while the more fertile meadows obviously attracted earlier settlers. Here are a number of solid farmsteads. One of the most attractive houses in Windlesham is Pound Cottage on Pound Lane. This timber-framed, 17th century cottage has a lovely thatched roof which comes down in hips to the ground floor ceiling.

Standing proudly along a rural country road in Windlesham is the ***Half Moon***, a traditional free house that is a favourite with locals and visitors alike. Traditional means just that, because the pub has been in the same family for nearly a century. The present owners, Conrad and Helga Sturt, ensure that there is always a warm welcome - including two open wood fireplaces blazing away in the winter. In the spring and summer customers can see why the Half Moon's gardens won the Pub category in the Surrey in Bloom competition, or they can walk in the privately run arboretum nearby. Theakstone's Old Peculiar and Bishop's Tipple are among the dozen or more classic English ales on tap. Helga's extensive menu includes fortifying dishes such as chicken and mushroom pie and steaks as well as lighter choices such as omelettes and filled jacket potatoes. The four-course Sunday lunch will set you up for the week. *The Half Moon, Church Road, Windlesham, Surrey GU20 6BN Tel: 01276 452023*

Lightwater *Map 2 ref C3*

7 miles W of Woking off the M3

For many Londoners, Lightwater represents the first taste of countryside outside the metropolis. It has the advantage - from the visitor's point of view - of lying within easy reach of the M3. By turning south off the motorway, instead of north to Bagshot, drivers soon enter a countryside defined by heaths and scattered woodlands. ***Bagshot Heath***, once a rough area peopled by highwaymen and duellists, begins at the western edge of Lightwater, and the bucolically named village of ***Donkey Town*** lies just to the south, its name providing some confirmation of the area's rural nature.

Just on the western edge of Lightwater, between Bagshot Heath to the north and the Military training area to the south is ***Lightwater and Heathland Visitor Centre***, a fascinating collection of exhibits about the history and natural history of this stretch of West Surrey countryside.

Camberley *Map 2 ref C4*

7 miles W of Woking off the M3

Prior to 1807, when the famous Sandhurst Royal Military Academy was relocated nearby, the substantial town of Camberley did not exist, and indeed its oldest part, the grid-patterned York Town, was constructed to house the academy's first instructors. (Lying just across the Berkshire border, Sandhurst Academy is set around a group of buildings designed in neoclassical style by James Wyatt.)

Although now resembling many other large towns with its High Street chains and modernised pubs, Camberley still displays much of the care and attention that marked its development in the mid-Victorian era. Unlike other towns which sprang up willy-nilly, usually with the advent of the railway, Camberley had a measured growth and the town expanded along the lines of the grid shape of York Town. Shops and workers' houses predominated north of the railway line while to the south were the larger houses of prosperous merchants set among stands of mature trees. These latter houses, many of which are good examples of the Arts and Crafts style of architect Norman Shaw and his followers, still stand although recent housing developments have encroached on much of the wooded areas.

The story of the development of Camberley and the surrounding area is well told at the ***Surrey Heath Museum*** on Knoll Road. Most of the exhibits have been designed to tell this story from a child's point of view, but adults will also enjoy seeing some of the curiosities and original documents from the 19th century. There are also displays on heathland crafts and the archaeology of the area.

Frimley — *Map 2 ref B4*

7 miles W of Woking off the M3

Frimley is an extremely old village on the Hampshire border and a site of several important prehistoric and Roman finds which are displayed at the Surrey Heath Museum in Camberley. Much of the more recent history, unfortunately, has been less well preserved and the old sense of the village's coaching significance has been erased with a series of housing developments over the last four decades. The area around ***Frimley Green***, however, gives some indication of what Frimley - and even its larger neighbour Camberley - looked like in the late medieval period. ***Cross Farmhouse*** is one of the oldest surviving houses, its timber-frame and brick structure containing elements dating from the 15th century. The parish church of St Peter dates only from 1825 but its churchyard contains the graves of many famous people. Among them is Francis Bret Harte, the American novelist whose wanderings around the world led him to settle eventually in England.

Just south of Frimley, and also hugging the Hampshire border, is the village of ***Mytchett***, which has also suffered from some unthinking urban planning. However, it does contain something of an imaginatively designed one-storey primary school which was built in the 1960s. In itself functional and not an attraction as such, Mytchett Primary School displays how modern construction can be achieved without pastiche and with an awareness of the special surroundings.

The Basingstoke Canal Visitors Centre, which lies just east of Farnborough and only five minutes from the M3, offers a tranquil and relaxing way in which to discover the charming countryside. Visitors can take a leisurely trip on a narrowboat, gaining a fasci-

Basingstoke Canal Visitors Centre

nating insight into the points of interest from the informative guide. The Canalside Tea Rooms and Gift Shop tempt people back on to dry land, while the Canal Exhibition provides an in-depth account of how barge skippers lived a century ago and how the Basingstoke Canal, and its wildlife habitats, have been conserved more recently. Children enjoy the adventure playground and pets corner. Many visitors take advantage of the Canal Explorer Ticket, which combines entrance to the canal exhibition, a boat cruise and a hot or cold drink and biscuits at the Canalside Tea Rooms. Rowing boats can be hired to explore the picturesque scenery along the canal. If you're taken with the area, you can stay at the adjacent campsite. *Basingstoke Canal Visitors Centre, Mytchett Place Road, Mytchett, Surrey GU16 6DD Tel: 01252 370073*

Farnborough *Map 2 ref C5*

7 miles W of Woking off A331

Farnborough lies just over the border in Hampshire and although it is largely a commercial and shopping - rather than historical - centre, it is worth visiting for its links with Royal Aircraft Establishment. These ties are explained fully at the ***RAMC*** and ***Royal Logistic Corps Museums*** which can also provide information about Farnborough's other claim to international fame, the annual Air Show.

Pirbright *Map 2 ref C5*

3 miles W of Woking on the A324

Pirbright is a village that is first recorded in 1166 as Perifrith, a compound of the two words "pyrige" (pear tree) and "fryth" (wooded country). It remained a hamlet of scattered homesteads until the 19th century when the railway's arrival in 1840 led to a boom in the population and a corresponding burgeoning of new construction.

Despite the rapid increase in the village population, and thanks also to the enlightened Green belt policies of this century, Pirbright has managed to keep most of its rural aspect. The huge village green which forms its core is in fact a wedge of the surrounding heathland. Pirbright contains many listed buildings, including several medieval farmsteads. Information about these, as well as a selection of excellent walks, is contained in a lovingly produced booklet available from the vicarage.

Extensive colourful gardens, frequent winners of the Guildford in Bloom festival, surround ***The Royal Oak***, an eighteenth-century pub set by a stream in the heart of Pirbright. Altogether, the setting and relaxed atmosphere strengthen the feeling of being in a rural hideaway, although the village of Pirbright lies handily between Woking and Aldershot. Manager Pauline Lay is proud of the

The Royal Oak

distinctive qualities of this welcoming pub, and even its recent extension incorporates an ancient oak door as well as pews and a stained glass window originally from a church. This thoughtfulness extends to the parking space reserved for the disabled - right at the front door. The Royal Oak is true to its roots, providing a wide range of real ales. The food, in keeping with other members of the collection of Wayside Inns, is of the highest standard, with hearty meals and traditional pies sharing menu space with sophisticated dishes such as salmon bernaise and Cannelloni provencale. *The Royal Oak, Aldershot Road, Pirbright, Surrey GU24 0DQ Tel: 01483 232466*

Standing at the edge of the Pirbright village green is ***The White Hart***. The pub has been an integral part of village life for centuries, often in unexpected ways. Don't be surprised to find a ghost or two while sipping a pint of real ale under the fine beamed ceilings - the cellar once served as a morgue. Highwaymen used the White Hart as an escape route; ask the friendly staff to show you where. Manager Yvonne Sanders manages to sneak in a number of modern conveniences without in any way disturbing the sense of history and

The White Hart

heritage. As part of the group of Big Steak Pubs, the White Hart serves a wide range of hearty dishes. Steak is an obvious choice, but there are other options to cater to vegetarians, children and fish lovers. The bread oven in the bar - yet more evidence of the pub's varied history - is where the tempting filled jacket potatoes are prepared. *The White Hart, The Green, Pirbright, Surrey GU24 0LP Tel: 01483 472366*

CHAPTER FOUR
Farnham and the West

The Granary, Peper Harrow Farm

Chapter 4 - Area Covered

For precise location of places please refer to the colour maps found at the rear of the book.

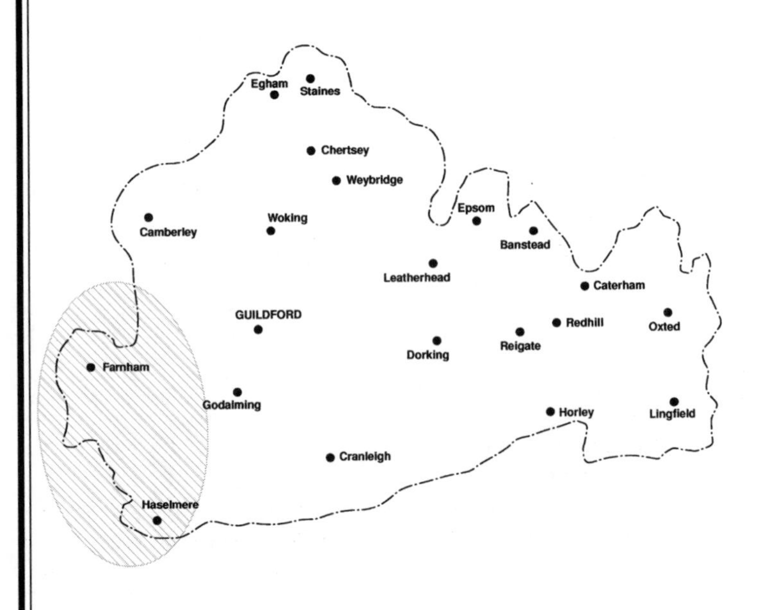

4
Farnham and the West

Introduction

Farnham, with its lovely Georgian architecture and battle-worn castle, is the largest town in southwestern Surrey, where the heel of the county extends westwards into Hampshire. Apart from Farnham, however, there are no large towns in this corner of the county, and its charms lie more in the array of attractive villages, scattered farmhouses, woodlands and open heaths in some of the hilliest parts of the Southeast.

History plays an important role in this area, with Civil War battle cries still almost audible from the walls of Farnham castle and the hint of plainsong hanging in the still air around the ruins of Waverley Abbey. "Stand and deliver" would seem to be a more appropriate sound to hear in the wilder sections of the southern extremity, and the Gibbet Memorial on Hindhead Common is a tangible reminder of the fate that awaited those highwaymen who had the misfortune to meet the long arm of the law.

The famous Hog's Back section of the A31 forms the northern edge of the area covered in this chapter. This lovely stretch of road is one of the most scenic drives in the Southeast, affording excellent views north and south as it traverses the ridge between Farnham and Guildford. Indeed, looking south from the Hog's Back provides an aerial perspective of many of the sites covered in the following pages, or at least the countryside surrounding them. The panorama is best viewed from the grassy verge by the side of the A31 at one of the many lay-bys.

Farnham

The most westerly town in Surrey is Farnham. This fine old settlement stands at the point where the old Pilgrims' Way from Winchester to Canterbury crosses the River Wey, and it has long been an important staging post on the busy trading route between Southampton and London. The town first became a residence of the Bishops of Winchester during Saxon times, and following the Norman conquest, the new Norman bishop built himself a castle on a pleasant tree-covered rise above the centre of the town. This impressive structure underwent a number of alterations, most notably in the 15th century when the decorated brick-built tower was added, and it remained in the hands of the Bishops of Winchester until 1927.

Farnham Castle has been visited on a number of occasions by the reigning English monarch and was besieged during the English Civil War. Today, it is approached along Castle Street, a delightful

Farnham Castle

wide thoroughfare of Georgian and neo-Georgian buildings which was laid out to accommodate a traditional street market. The old Norman keep, now owned by English Heritage, is open daily, 10.00

to 18.00pm between 1 April and 30 September. The remainder of the castle, including the Great Hall, can be visited on Wednesdays only between 14.00 and 16.00 throughout the year.

Farnham contains a number of other interesting historic buildings, including a row of 17th century gabled almshouses and Willmer House in West Street, a handsome Georgian-fronted structure which now houses the informative ***Farnham Museum***. As well as some fine wood panelling, carvings and period furniture, the museum contains some interesting archaeological exhibits and a unique collection of 19th century glass paperweights.

Farnham Maltings in Bridge Square is a thriving arts and community centre which is housed in a listed early 18th century commercial building. As well as an excellent cafe and bar, the centre offers a regular programme of live music, films and exhibitions. Another good place to see a show or enjoy a meal is Farnham's ***Redgrave Theatre*** in Brightwells.

Annies Antiques, a corner shop at the outskirts of Farnham, is the sort of fascinating place that seems to change by the day. One day it might be full of Victorian paintings and furniture, just waiting for the antimacassars to complete the set. The next could find a treasure trove of art deco lamps and clocks, all streamlined angles and chrome. Annie has an eye for the unusual, and she is a trader in the friendly, old-fashioned sense. Walk in with an item and she will probably make you an offer - and you might walk out with that unusual antique that you never knew you wanted but now you can't live without. A steady stream of customers is proof that Annie knows her stuff, and that locals know where to go when they are looking

Annies Antiques

for quality antiques or simply amusing bric-a-brac. Much of the stock comes from house clearances, and customers can spend hours trying to match the intriguing items with the sort of person who once owned them. *Annies Antiques, 1 Ridgway Parade, Farnham, Surrey GU9 8JN Tel: 01252 713447/723217*

Heath Lodge, owned and run by Barbara and Martin Jones, offers comfortable bed and breakfast accommodation in a period house just a mile and half south of Farnham and its Georgian attractions. The house, which is on a quiet road, is Edwardian but some of its upper features are more than three centuries old. Inside this no-smoking house the atmosphere is relaxing and welcoming, and an impressive grandfather clock, old photographs and period furnishings set off Barbara's impressive collection of ornamental boxes. The two guest rooms are bright and comfortable, adding to the homely feel of Heath Lodge. A sunny, south-facing drawing room looks out on the mature tree-lined garden with its beautiful roses. Heath Lodge provides an excellent base for exploring historic Farnham or the Wey Valley and Surrey-Hampshire border, and the Joneses are happy to impart some of the insider's knowledge they have picked up in the ten years they have spent at Heath Lodge. *Heath Lodge, 91a Shortheath Road, Farnham, Surrey GU9 8SF Tel: 01252 722918*

Heath Lodge

By taking Sandrock Hill Road out of Farnham you soon leave the hurly-burly of the modern world and begin to enter wooded countryside that has more than its share of genuine attractions, such as ***The Sandrock***. Here is a pub that lives up to its inclusion in this book as a hidden gem; it stands guard on the side of the quiet road, its entrance framed by potted plants, hanging baskets and window boxes. Just as importantly - to those with a love of old pubs and a

The Sandrock

thirst for real ales - it more than justifies its description as a free house, or, as owners Andrew and Caroline Baylis put it, "a house of Ale repute". Despite their punning, the Baylises take the job of providing excellent beers seriously, and you'll have a chance to sample Bathams, Timothy Taylors and at least six other guest beers, many of them from local breweries. There is also a chance to have a bar meal or simply a roll while you consider the next round. *The Sandrock, Sandrock Hill Road, Farnham, Surrey GU10 4NS Tel: 01252 715865*

East to the Hog's Back

Waverley Abbey *Map 2 ref B7*

2 miles E of Farnham on the B3001

Lying within easy striking distance of Farnham are the atmospheric ruins of Waverley Abbey. Dating from the 12th century, this was the first Cistercian abbey to be built in England. The first church was completed in 1160 and destroyed during the dissolution of the monasteries. Its monumental floor plan was only revealed after excavations this century. Although there is little in the way of architectural detail recognisable to the untrained eye, architectural historians have suggested that this early church might well have inspired the famous Gothic churches of Tintern, Fountains and Riveaulx abbeys, so the decline of Waverley takes on a sadder aspect.

Waverley Abbey

The Abbey remains are open during daylight hours and are said to have provided the inspiration for Sir Walter Scott's romantic novel, Waverley, published in 1814 during his stay at the nearby ***Waverley Abbey House*** whose imposing structure was built with stone taken from the abbey in 1723.

Close by lies ***The Barley Mow,*** a traditional whitewashed country pub that deserves to be described as a hidden gem. Located just east of Farnham, and within easy reach of Guildford and Godalming, it lies on a rural road and is surrounded by miles of unspoilt coun-

The Barley Mow

tryside. There is a timeless, tranquil look to the pub, which is also evident in the mellow interior. Owner Paul Evans provides a hearty welcome and augments the liquid refreshments with a wide variety of enticing food. The home-prepared food on the extensive menu ranges from light snacks in the "pub grub" vein to more substantial fare to satisfy the walkers and cyclists who frequent the pub. In fact several marked country walks actually set off from the Barely Mow. Those with a less energetic disposition can still enjoy the countryside at one of the tables in the colourful garden, with its views of the woods and fields beyond. *The Barley Mow, The Sands, near Farnham, Surrey GU10 1NE Tel: 01252 782200*

Tilford

Map 2 ref B7

3 miles E of Farnham off the B3001

A lovely two mile riverside walk from Waverley Abbey leads to Tilford, an attractive village which stands at the confluence of the two branches of the River Wey. The monks of Waverley are believed to have been responsible for rebuilding Tilford's two medieval bridges following the devastating floods of 1233 during which the abbey itself had to be evacuated. At the heart of Tilford stands a triangular village green which features a 900 year old oak tree with a 25 foot girth which is known as the King's or Novel's Oak; a pleasant early 18th century inn can be found nearby. Tilford's parish church of All Saints hosts a regular spring festival of early church music.

In Reeds Road to the southwest of Tilford is the ***Rural Life Centre*** and ***Old Kiln Museum***, which contains an interesting display of historic agricultural equipment and rural memorabilia, along with working blacksmith's and wheelwright's workshops. The museum spreads over 10 acres of field, woodland, and barns and there is even a narrow gauge railway.

Runfold

Map 2 ref B6

2 miles E of Farnham on the A31

Runfold marks the beginning of the large tracts of woodland that dominate much of the landscape between Farnham and Guildford. A well-marked turning off the A31 indicates the small road that winds south into the village. Runfold, like its immediate - and even smaller - neighbour Seale, was essentially a mixed farming community in the medieval period, and this way of life is displayed in Manor Farm, which lies between the two villages.

The Princess Royal, run by Geoff Lackford, is a roadside pub that was built in 1938 to capture passing trade from motorists on their way through Runfold on the main Guildford to Farnham road.

The Princess Royal

Its name refers to Princess Mary, the Princess Royal at the time. The recently built Farnham Bypass, however, has siphoned off much of the traffic and has changed the role of this free house. With the traffic flow at an ebb, the Princess Royal has concentrated on building a reputation for its restaurant and on making itself a base for walks in the rolling countryside. Ordnance Survey maps, pored over by eager ramblers, are a common sight in the garden to the rear. Walkers - or anyone with a good appetite and a taste for well-prepared food - can choose from a varied menu influenced by French, Cajun, Chinese and Indian cuisines. As befits the pub's name, there is even a nod to royalty: Salmon Balmoral comes in a lobster and brandy cream sauce. *The Princess Royal, Guildford Road, Runfold, Farnham, Surrey GU10 1NX Tel: 01252 782243*

Tongham

Map 2 ref C6

2 miles E of Farnham on the A31

Tongham lies at an important junction, where Surrey meets Hampshire. Aldershot lies just west across the border which is marked by the A331. With the busy A31, linking Farnham and Guildford lying just to the south, Tongham is hard pressed to retain any sense of the country. That it manages to is to the credit of the planners, who have ensured that many of its timber-framed cottages are still seen to good effect. Look out for the distinctive curved braces (the timbers linking walls and roof) on some of these cottages. Tongham boasts its own brewery called the ***Hogs Back Brewery*** after the hill to the east of the town and the stretch of the A30 that continues to Guildford. It is famous for its TEA (or Traditional English Ale) and is based in farm buildings on The Street, just off the A30 out of Farnham.

Hog'sBack — *Map 2 ref C6*

3-8 miles E of Farnham on the A31

The Hog's Back is the name given to the ridge which dominates the landscape between the level ground surrounding Guildford (looking north) and the wooded, more undulating terrain looking south towards Hindhead. Motorists refer to this stretch of the A31 as the Hog's Back, and the 4 mile stretch between Tongham and Compton is well served with picnic stops and the occasional lay-by to stop and admire the views.

The hamlet of ***Wanborough*** on the northern side of the A31 contains one of the smallest churches in Surrey. Built by the monks of Waverley Abbey, it stands in the shadow of a massive monastic tithe barn.

The old manor house was constructed between the 15th and 17th centuries on the site of pre-Norman manor and was used during World War II to train secret agents.

Puttenham — *Map 2 ref C6*

5 miles E of Farnham off the A31

The Hog's Back village of Puttenham lies stretched out along the route of the old Pilgrims' Way. An attractive mixture of building styles, the village contains a restored part-Norman church, several fine 15th and 16th century cottages, an 18th century farm with a number of period outbuildings and oast houses, and an impressive Palladian mansion, ***Puttenham Priory***, which was completed in 1762.

The mixture of building styles arose because of Puttenham's location, where chalk gives way to sandstone. Cottages use one or the other - or both - of these materials, and the effect is enlivened with brickwork usually dating from the 18th century.

Elstead — *Map 2 ref C7*

5 miles E of Farnham on the B3001

The attractive village of Elstead lies surrounded by farmland and crossed by the River Wey. In fact it is this crossing that makes Elstead noteworthy. Its rough stonework bridge dates from the medieval period, crossing the river in a series of five graceful arches. It has a brick parapet, making the overall effect one of solidity and strength. Unfortunately, the medieval effect is lessened somewhat by the modern bridge that runs parallel to it on the north side. Nevertheless, the bridge marks a delightful entrance to the village itself.

On the lane leading from the old bridge to the village green is the ***Old Farm House***, a large timber-framed building that was completed in the 16th century. The green itself is compact and triangular and a small cul-de-sac leads from it to the 14th century Church of St James, which was overly restored in the 19th century.

Just west of the centre is ***Elstead Mill***, an 18th century water mill. It stands four storeys high, its brick structure topped with a Palladian cupola. Six classical columns support a small lead dome at the very top.

Peper Harow

Map 2 ref C7

6 miles E of Farnham off the A3

Peper Harow is a small village lying just west of the A3 in completely rural surroundings. It has a number of interesting cottages reinforcing its rustic charm as well as one of the best collections of Surrey farm buildings at ***Peper Harow Farm*** just outside the centre of the village. Of particular interest is the large granary, built

The Granary, Peper Harow Farm

around 1600. It stands - resting on its 25 wooden pillars - at the centre of a quadrangle at the heart of the farm.

The ***Church of St Nicholas***, in the centre of the village, was built in Norman times but was massively restored in the 19th century. The restoration, however, was conducted by A W N Pugin, and there is great care evident throughout. St Nicholas represents something of a find for students of architecture since it appear to be one of the few churches where Pugin sought to create a Neo-Norman effect; most of his work strove for the higher-flown Gothic styles.

The other big attraction in the village is ***Peper Harow House***, a cube-shaped manor house completed in 1768. The bottom two storeys are soberly classical but an extra floor was added in 1913 along with some Baroque ornamentation that clashes with the style of the original building. The outbuildings are almost as impressive as the house itself, in particular the three-sided stables. The park surrounding the house was designed by Capability Brown in 1763.

South to Hindhead

Frensham

Map 2 ref B7

3 miles S of Farnham off the A28

In Frensham, ***St Mary's Church*** contains a large medieval copper cauldron whose history is surrounded in legend. According to one story, it was lent by the fairies to a human who held onto it for longer than was agreed; when it was finally returned, the fairies refused to accept it, vowing never again lend anything to human beings. Another story tells how the cauldron once belonged to Mother Ludlam, a local witch-like character who inhabited a cave near Waverley Abbey.

The village of ***Millbridge*** lies just to the north of Frensham, and like Frensham it is set in heaths with occasional farmland dotted around it. This provides an ideal setting for the ***Rural Life Centre***, which provides insights and a number of hands-on exhibits relating to the farming history of western Surrey and its heathland.

The Frensham Garden Centre is located, appropriately enough, just a few hundred yards along from the Rural Life Centre in Frensham. These peaceful surroundings are enough to stir the soul of even the most inexperienced plantsman and the centre caters for a wide range of gardening needs. The well-stocked plant section provides a selection of trees, shrubs, alpines, roses, climbers and hedging plants along with more seasonal items such as bedding and herbaceous plants, herbs and soft fruit bushes. The garden centre shop and furniture section are equally well stocked, with products to fit nearly every gardening occasion. Thousands of "teasel people" welcome customers to the craft shop, with its wealth of gift ideas stemming from traditional handicrafts. When it is time to pore over

The Frensham Garden Centre

the purchases, or simply to gather energy for more browsing, customers can visit Beatons Coffee and Tea Shop. The coffee shop, like the centre, is open daily, and has been awarded the Tea Council Award for Excellence. *Frensham Garden Centre, The Reeds, Frensham, Surrey GU10 3BP Tel: 01252 792545*

The Mariners Hotel enjoys a tranquil setting by the River Wey in Frensham. Owner Carlo Genziani has been running the hotel for 15 years, and the results are a testimony to his experience and attention to detail. The 21 rooms are all en-suite and equipped to ac-

The Mariners Hotel

commodate all manner of special visitor - the disabled, young parents, bridal couples or anyone who needs to feel pampered for a night or a weekend break. The bistro-style restaurant has an Italian flavour, with an excellent range of pizza and pasta along with specialities, particularly fish. The lounge, with its cosy log fire, is the place for a pint of real ale and a lighter meal, while in the summer, guests can enjoy a barbecue outside on the terrace. The hotel is set in unspoilt countryside, and many guests take advantage of the opportunities nearby to golf, fish, ride or simply amble through the National Trust parkland which is close at hand. *The Mariners Hotel, Millbridge, Frensham, Farnham, Surrey GU10 3DJ Tel: 01252 792050/794745, Fax: 01252 792649*

The A287 to the south of the village runs between Frensham's ***Great and Little Ponds***, two sizeable National Trust-owned lakes which provide good bird-watching and recreational facilities. These are now contained within a 1,000 acre country park which incorporates four prehistoric bowl barrows and the ***Devil's Jumps***, three irregularly shaped hills whose origin, like many other unusual natural features, is attributed to Satan.

Thursley *Map 2 ref C7*

6 miles SE of Farnham off the A3

Thursley is an exceptional village which takes its name from the Viking god Thor and the Saxon word for field, or lea. The settlement was once an important centre of the Wealden iron industry and number of disused hammer ponds can still be seen to the east. These artificial lakes provided power to drive the mechanical hammers and bellows in the once-bustling iron forges. Today, the village is a tranquil place arranged around a green containing an acacia tree which was planted as a memorial to William Cobbett, the Georgian traveller and writer who is best remembered for his book describing riding tours of England, *"Rural Rides"*, which was published in 1830. Thursley is also the birthplace of the celebrated architect, Sir Edwin Lutyens, who at the age of only nineteen converted a row of local cottages into a single dwelling now known as the Corner.

Thursley's two principal thoroughfares, the Lane and the Street, contain a wide variety of noteworthy domestic buildings. The latter leads to ***St Michael's Church***, a part-Saxon structure which was heavily restored by the Victorians. The spire and belfry are 15th century and are supported by massive timber posts with tie-beams and arched braces, a good example of late-medieval engineering.

Thursley Church

The churchyard contains the grave of a sailor, who was murdered on Hindhead Heath in 1786 by three men he had gone to help. Although the villagers never discovered the victim's name, they gave him a full burial and erected an inscribed stone over his grave.

Two interesting old buildings stand near the church, the half-timbered and tile-hung Old Parsonage and the part timber framed Hill Farm, both of which date from the 16th century.

The Devil's Punch Bowl *Map 2 ref C8*

7 miles SE of Farnham off the A3

The Devil's Punch Bowl is a steep-sided natural sandstone amphitheatre through which the busy A3 Guildford to Petersfield road passes four miles to the southeast of Frensham Great Pond. As usual, Lucifer's name is invoked in the place name but the origins might have more to do with real events than with superstition. The deep valley provided excellent cover for thieves and highwaymen, and even in coaching days passengers would look on the natural wonder with a mixture of awe and apprehension.

Hindhead *Map 2 ref B8*

7 miles S of Farnham on the A28

Hindhead stands near the top of a ridge and at 850 feet above sea level, is the highest village in Surrey. Perhaps surprisingly, it has only been in existence since the late 19th century. Before that the site was known primarily as a site for highwaymen planning their next heist while taking cover in the steep wooded countryside. Good stands of fir trees still surround Hindhead.

The town grew up along the Portsmouth Road (now the A3) and the buildings date mainly from a concentrated period in the 1890s. Shops were built along the Portsmouth Road and a number of comfortable residences were dotted through the surrounding woodlands. Most of these houses still enjoy leafy settings even if today the appearance is somewhat tamer. The late 1890s construction date means that these residences enjoyed the benefit of the Arts and Crafts movement; most of them derive from the designs of Norman Shaw, the movement's great proponent. One of the best examples of this style is ***Thirlestane*** on the Farnham Road. Making the most of the south-facing situation, as well as the height, this V-shaped house faces southwest so that most of it acts as a suntrap. A deliberately rough exterior, combined with the hanging tiles, typify the attention to quality materials while the deliberately asymmetrical nature of the two wings suggests the freedom of spirit that is associated with that period.

Hindhead Common *Map 2 ref C8*

7 miles SE of Farnham off the A3

Lying just to the east of Hindhead itself is Hindhead Common, comprising a largely untamed collection of wild heathlands, pinewoods and steep valleys. The National Trust owns 1,400 acres of Hindhead Common, and maintains a series of trails and paths that takes visitors through evocatively named sites such as Polecat Copse, Golden Valley, Hurt Hill and Stoatley Green. On the summit of ***Gibbet Hill*** is a granite monument marking the spot where the gibbet stood. The glorious views across both the North and South Downs was the last earthly memory of the thieves and murderers who were executed here.

CHAPTER FIVE
Guildford and the South

Tigbourne Court

Chapter 5 - Area Covered

For precise location of places please refer to the colour maps found at the rear of the book.

5
Guildford and the South

Introduction

Guildford, with its prominent setting on a hill visible from the A3, is an obvious base for travellers interested in exploring the southwestern section of Surrey that extends down to and then traces the West Sussex border. Like the area around Farnham, this area contains some of Surrey's most unspoilt countryside. Rough, hilly, thickly wooded in places, the landscape comes as close as anywhere in the county to fitting the descriptive term "wild".

The interaction between landscape and human society provides the background for some of the most interesting sights covered in the following pages. From time-worn remnants of prehistoric hill forts to medieval bridges along the Wey Valley and even including some of the modern architecture to be found among Guildford's hilly streets, the imprint of necessity-driven design is everywhere. Is it any wonder that Sir Edwin Lutyens cut his teeth, architecturally speaking, with his designs for houses occupying hilly sites or tucked in narrow valleys?

The settlements become decidedly smaller and more scattered as the Sussex border is neared. It is in these villages, many no more than hamlets, that visitors can appreciate just how even the earliest settlers scraped a living, and how later inhabitants developed crafts that exploited the rich natural surroundings.

Guildford

The route into Guildford from the northwest passes close to ***Guildford Cathedral***, one of only two new Anglican cathedrals to have been built in this country since the Reformation (the other is Liverpool). This impressive redbrick building stands on top of Stag Hill, a prominent local landmark which enjoys panoramic views over the surrounding landscape. The building was designed by Sir Edward Maufe with a superb high-arched interior and was begun in 1936. However, work was halted during World War II and members of the local diocese had to wait until 1961 for the new cathedral to be finally consecrated. Guided tours and restaurant facilities are available all year round. In 1968, the ***University of Surrey*** relocated from London to a site on a hillside to the northwest of the cathedral. Pleasant and leafy, the campus contains a number of striking buildings including the university library and art gallery.

From the university, it is only a mile to the heart of Guildford, the ancient county town of Surrey. Guildford has been the capital of the region since pre-Norman times and in the 10th century, it even had its own mint. Henry II built a ***Castle*** here on high ground in the 12th century which later became the county gaol; today, the castle remains house a renowned brass-rubbing centre and the ruined keep provides a fascinating place from which to view the surrounding area.

Guildhall, Guildford

Those visiting the town for the first time should make straight for the old ***High Street***, a wonderful cobbled thoroughfare of Georgian and older buildings which rises steeply from the River Wey. Perhaps the most noteworthy of these is the ***Guildhall***, a

Tudor structure with an elaborately decorated 17th century frontage which incorporates a belltower, balcony and distinctive gilded clock.

Abbot's Hospital, a little further along, is an imposing turreted almshouse which was built in 1619 by the Guildford-born Archbishop of Canterbury, George Abbot; at the top of the High Street, the ***Royal Grammar School*** dates from the early 1500s and was subsequently endowed by Edward VI.

A number of interesting streets and alleyways run off Guildford High Street, including Quarry Street with its mediaeval St Mary's Church and old Castle Arch. The latter houses the ***Guildford Museum***, an informative centre for local history and archaeology which also contains an exhibition devoted to Lewis Carroll, the creator of *"Alice In Wonderland"* who died in the town in 1898.

A charming bronze memorial to Lewis Carroll (real name Charles Lutwidge Dodgson) which is composed of a life-sized Alice chasing the White Rabbit into his hole can be found on the far bank of the River Wey, midway between the two footbridges. The famous ***Yvonne Arnaud Theatre*** stands in a delightful riverside setting at the foot of the castle mound on the town side of the river. As well as offering top quality productions, the theatre has an excellent bar, coffee lounge and restaurant which remains open throughout the day. In summer, rowing boats and guided pleasure boat trips are available at the nearby Guildford Boat House.

For all its attractions, Guildford can seem a bit too bustling to house many hidden places, but ***The Royal Oak*** pub is there to con-

The Royal Oak

found such expectations. This popular local, known simply as "the Oak", is tucked away in the pleasant hamlet of Wood Street Village on the outskirts of Guildford. It is the sort of place where customers happily shift down a few gears when they enter, and where you'll hear the clicking of dominoes rather than the incessant bass line of the latest pop hit. Tony Oliver is a popular landlord, so much so that he brought a number of regular customers with him when he recently took over the Royal Oak. It's worth taking your time to explore the food choices carefully; sharing space on the menu with traditional favourites such as steak and mushroom pie and ploughman's lunches are more exotic choices such as chicken jalfreezi, Bombay potatoes and Toulouse sausages. *The Royal Oak, 89 Oak Hill, Wood Street Village, Guildford, Surrey GU3 3DA Tel: 01483 235137*

Around Guildford

Clandon Park — *Map 2 ref E5*

5 miles E of Guildford on the A247

Set in the farming countryside east of Guildford and south of Woking is the National Trust-owned property, ***Clandon Park***. This magnificent country mansion was designed in the 1730s by Giacomo Leoni, a Venetian architect who combined Palladian, Baroque and European styles to create one of the grandest 18th century houses in England. The interior is renowned for its magnificent two-storey marble hall, sumptuous decoration and fine Italian plasterwork depicting scenes from mythology. The Gubbay collection of furniture and porcelain is also housed here, along with the Ivo Forde collection of humorous Meissen figures. The surrounding parkland was landscaped by Capability Brown in characteristic style and includes a parterre, grotto and brightly painted New Zealand Maori house.

Gomshall — *Map 3 ref F6*

5 miles E of Guildford on the A25

This once-industrialised community has a Victorian heart and was once an important centre of the tanning and leather-working industries. The old packhorse bridge over the River Tillingbourne dates from the 1500s and the manor house at the southern end of the village from the early 1700s. Gomshall is now known for its fine craft and antique shops, several of which are concentrated in an ancient and beautifully converted water mill, the ***Gomshall Mill and Gallery***. This working water mill dates back to 1086 and now houses attractive and unusual shops, a tea room and a licensed restaurant.

Shere

Map 3 ref F6

6 miles E of Guildford off the A25

Shere is one of the loveliest, and consequently most visited, villages in Surrey. Thankfully now bypassed by the A25, it lies at the foot of the North Downs in the river valley which is particularly known for the growing of watercress, a plant that requires a constantly flowing supply of fresh water. The village ***Church of St James*** dates from the 12th century and was tastefully restored in the 1950s. Among its many noteworthy features are the 13th century Purbeck marble font, the St Nicholas Chapel, and an unusual hermit's cell built in the 14th century for a local woman who asked to be confined there for life.

The churchyard is entered through an impressive lych gate designed by Lutyens and close by stands the White Horse Inn, one of the many fine 16th and 17th century buildings to be found in the village. The ***Shere Museum*** in the Malt House contains an interesting collection of local artefacts, and the ***Old Farm*** behind the church is an open farm which at weekends offers hands-on demonstrations of traditional farming techniques.

Albury

Map 3 ref E6

4 miles E of Guildford on the A28

Albury dates largely from the last century and was constructed in fanciful neo-Gothic style as an estate village for nearby ***Albury Park***. This large country mansion was built on the site of a Tudor manor house in the early 18th century and was much altered by Pugin in the 1840s. The most eccentric feature of the house is its collection of chimneys, 63 of them built for only 60 rooms in an amazing variety of shapes and sizes. Although the mansion has now been converted into flats, the estate gardens are open to visitors and are well worth a look. They were laid out by the diarist John Evelyn at the turn of the 18th century and feature a series of terraced orchards which rise above the house to the north. A number of smaller communities nestle around Albury.

Nearby, the tranquil hamlet of Albury Heath is the home of ***The King William IV*** pub, which is a marvellous window on to the past. Oddly enough, the pub predates its namesake by 300 years, and the interior is an oak-beamed indication that this inn goes back

King William IV

600 years. These beams can be low in places - fourteenth-century customers were shorter than today's clientele - so don't knock your head. Blazing fires crackle in the winter while the sun-dappled garden makes a lovely spot to take time out in the warmer months. Mike Davids is a welcoming host, and his cooking is a testimony to years working in the Army Catering Corps, preparing food for the officer's mess. The menu changes regularly but often features a full Sunday breakfast for the outdoor types who love this leafy part of Surrey. To top it off, the King William IV is a free house, and there is a wide range of ales to slake your thirst or to wash down a meal. *King William IV, Little London, Albury Heath, Surrey Tel: 01483 202685*

Chilworth — *Map 3 ref E6*

3 miles E of Guildford on the A28

Chilworth is a former munitions and paper-making centre whose church, ***St Martha on the Hill***, had to be rebuilt in 1850 following an explosion in the nearby gunpowder works. The result is a genuine success and shows great flair and sensitivity. There was no attempt made to copy the original exactly but the resulting reconstruction remains true to the Norman spirit of the destroyed church. On the hill to the south of the church are five circular banks, about 100 feet in diameter, which have been identified as early Bronze Age henge monuments.

Chilworth Manor was built in the 1600s on the site of a pre-Norman monastic house. The exterior is a medley of styles but its 17th century gardens are complete, running up the side of the hill in terraces.

Shalford *Map 2 ref D6*

3 miles S of Guildford on the A281

The residential community of Shalford contains a fascinating ***Water Mill*** which operated from the early 1700s right up to the First World War. Once powered by the waters of the Tillingbourne, this exceptional tile-hung structure retains most of its original machinery. During the 1930s, it was bought and restored by Ferguson's Gang, a secretive group of conservationists who hid their identities behind eccentric noms de plume and who eventually donated the building to the National Trust.

Shalford stands near the northern entrance to the ***Wey and Arun Junction Canal***, an ambitious inland waterway which was constructed in 1816 to connect the Thames with the English Channel. Conceived during the Napoleonic wars as a way of avoiding attacks on coastal shipping, unfortunately it opened too late to fulfil its function and was soon superseded by the railways. A towpath providing some delightful walks runs along almost two-thirds of the canal's 36 mile length, a significant proportion of which has now be restored by enthusiastic teams of volunteers.

About a mile south of Shalford is ***Great Tangley***, one of the finest 16th century half-timbered houses in Surrey. The exterior is made up of roughly square panels each with four curved diagonal braces. This combination creates a star shape for each panel, which is repeated across the sides of the house.

Blackheath *Map 3 ref E6*

4 miles SE of Guildford off the A248

Set in the hills above Albury, this tidy Victorian hamlet gives the visitor a sense of remoteness despite being within easy striking distance of Guildford. Blackheath has some fine late-Victorian buildings. One of the most interesting is ***Greyfriars***, a Franciscan monastery built in neo-Gothic style in 1895. The church and dormitories of this stone-built structure are contained under one roof. Another Victorian curiosity is the somewhat austere timbered residence, the Hallams.

Wonersh *Map 3 ref E6*

4 miles SE of Guildford off the A248

Wonersh is a former weaving centre with a fine 16th-century half-timbered inn, the Grantley Arms, located along the high street, which presents a cheerful and harmonious appearance with its medley of brick, stone, tile-hanging and half-timbered buildings. An imposing Lutyens house, ***Chinthurst Hill***, is just a few minutes' walk northwest of the heart of the village. Lutyens used the local Bargate stone to create a Tudor effect, this being between 1893 and 1895, before he had developed his own distinctive style. The house occupies a lovely hillside site and the terraced garden was planted by Gertrude Jekyll.

Bramley *Map 2 ref D6*

3 miles SE of Guildford off the A248

Despite being largely Victorian, Bramley has some attractive Georgian and Regency residential buildings. These appear somewhat haphazardly through the long winding street that forms the nearest thing to a core of the village. There are two Lutyens houses in Bramley. The small, L-shaped ***Millmead***, a National Trust property, is located south of Gosden Green. It was built for the gardener Gertrude Jekyll between 1904 and 1907 and traces of her original garden survive. About half a mile north is ***Little Tangley***, a late 19th century house to which Lutyens added a porch and staircase hall in 1899. The Stables, which are now a private house called Edgton, was one of the architect's first works.

Godalming *Map 2 ref D7*

5 miles S of Guildford on the A3100

The old market town of Godalming was once an important staging post between London and Portsmouth and a number of elegant 17th and 18th century shops and coaching inns can still be found in the High Street. A market was established here in 1300 and the town later became a centre for the local wool and textile industries. Perhaps the most interesting building in the old centre is the ***Pepperpot***, the former town hall which was built at the western end of the High Street in 1814. Now surrounded on all sides by heavy traffic, this unusual arcaded building once contained an interesting ***museum of local history*** which has recently moved to new premises at 109a High Street

Godalming's part-Norman parish church of St Peter and St Paul is built of Bargate stone, a locally quarried hard brown sandstone that was much-loved by the Victorians. This material was also used extensively to build ***Charterhouse School***, the famous public school which moved from London to a hillside site on the northern side of Godalming in 1872. Among its most striking features are the 150 foot Founder's Tower and the chapel designed by Giles Gilbert Scott as a memorial to those killed in the First World War. The timber-framed house once belonging to Gertrude Jekyll can be found in dense woodland on the opposite side of town; it was designed for her by Edwin Lutyens in characteristic rural vernacular style and partially constructed of Bargate stone.

Located just a few miles south of Guildford and just off the A3 is ***The Squirrel at Hurtmore***, a bar-restaurant and country hotel which offers the chance to unwind in an atmosphere of comfort and attentive service. The Squirrel comprises the table d'hôte restaurant, brasserie and five guest rooms in the main building - and an additional eight guest rooms in a row of restored seventeenth century cottages. Jordy Vazquez, the owner since 1994, is a skilled restaurateur with vast experience at some of the best London res-

The Squirrel at Hurtmore

taurants, including the Savoy, the Connaught and Crockfords. This experience is particularly evident in the restaurant, which features the best cuisine from the UK and Europe and is backed up by an extensive wine list. Its conservatory has a continental feel. The brasserie is a cosy and relaxed area, with Spanish plates hanging on the walls behind the comfortable settees and chairs, offering a wide range of lighter meals. The bar has a good choice of real ales, wines and spirits and in the warmer weather patrons can eat and drink outside on the veranda in the garden.

The accommodation has the same caring touch, with each room having a distinctive feel, although all are equipped to a high standard. Those in the cottages have a real sense of yesteryear, with their steep stairs and wooden beams. There is even an example of the original wattle and daub wall on display. Children are made especially welcome at the Squirrel and there is a special children's menu. Children love the swings, slide, Wendy house and bouncy castle in

Cottages, The Squirrel at Hurtmore

the spacious garden where the barbecue operating on summer weekends is another popular attraction. The Squirrel is conveniently located next to Hurtmore Golf Course and there are many country walks and cycle routes through the adjacent countryside. *The Squirrel at Hurtmore, Hurtmore, Godalming, Surrey GU7 2RN Tel 01483 860223, Fax: 01483 860592*

Three miles along the B2130 to the southeast of Godalming lies the renowned ***Winkworth Arboretum***, a 95 acre area of wooded hillside which was presented to the National Trust in 1952. The grounds contain two lakes and a magnificent collection of rare trees and shrubs, many of them native to other continents. ***Hascombe***, one mile further on, is another characteristic Surrey village with great charm.

Loseley Park — *Map 2 ref D6*

3 miles N of Godalming off the B3000

Loseley Park, a handsome Elizabethan country estate, was built in 1562 of Bargate stone, some of which was taken from the ruins of Waverley Abbey. Loseley House is the former home of the Elizabethan statesman, Sir William More. Both Elizabeth I and James I are known to have stayed here, and the interior is decorated with a series of outstanding period features, including hand-painted panelling, woodcarving, delicate plasterwork ceilings, and a unique chimney-piece carved from a massive piece of chalk. The walled garden is a beautiful place to take a stroll, the surrounding gardens contain a terrace and a moat walk, and the nearby fields are home to Loseley's famous herd of pedigree Jersey cattle. Visitors can take a trailer ride to the traditional working dairy farm, where you can see the

Jersey herd being milked every afternoon and discover the history of the estate.

Compton *Map 2 ref D6*

4 miles N of Godalming off the B3000

The historic community of Compton was once an important stopping place on the old Pilgrims' Way. The village possesses an exceptional part-Saxon church, St Nicholas, with some remarkable internal features, including a series of 12th century murals which were only rediscovered in 1966, an ancient hermit's, or anchorite's, cell, and a unique two-storey Romanesque sanctuary which is thought to have once contained an early Christian relic.

Compton is also renowned for being the home of the 19th century artist G F Watts, a chiefly self-taught painter and sculptor whose most famous work, *Physical Energy*, stands in London's Kensington Gardens. At the age of 47, Watts married the actress Ellen Terry, but the couple separated a year later; then at the age of 69, he successfully remarried, this time to Mary Fraser-Tytler, a painter and potter 33 years his junior who went on to design ***Watts' Memorial Gallery***, which today contains over 200 pieces of the artist's work, along with the ***Watts Mortuary Chapel***, an extraordinary building which was completed in 1904 and is decorated in exuberant Art Nouveau style. The Watts Gallery is a fascinating place to visit, housing a unique collection of his paintings, drawings and sculptures. The nearby memorial chapel is also worth visiting.

Just on the edge of the attractive village of Compton, and only three miles from the centre of Guildford, is ***Little Polsted***, which offers bed and breakfast accommodation in a charming cottage at

Little Polstead

the end of the garden. Breakfast is served in the main house, where there is also ample parking space. The Walkinshaws, who own Little Polsted, are only too happy to tell guests about the history of the cottage, which is an elegantly converted pump house. The two guest rooms in the quiet and secluded cottage contain a good range of period furnishings and enjoy fine views over the surrounding farmland. This rural setting attracts visitors who enjoy walking, bird-watching or simply soaking up the atmosphere of Compton, a village that seems unchanged in over two centuries. As a result, Little Polsted has more than its share of repeat visitors, so it is worth booking in advance. *Little Polsted, Polsted Lane, Compton, Guildford, Surrey GU3 1JE Tel/fax: 01483 810398*

South to the Sussex Border

Eashing

Map 2 ref D7

1 mile W of Godalming off the A3100

The tiny hamlet of Eashing is noted for the lovely medieval ***Eashing Bridge***, which has segmented arches and uses cutwaters - pointed upstream and rounded downstream to stem the flow of the river. It is one of several surviving Wey Valley bridges of that period, the others being at Elstead and Tilford. Just to the east of the bridge is The Meads, an ancient house of two distinct parts. Half of it is 16th century, with timber framing and an original Tudor doorcase. The other is 18th century and brick and stone, with small dark chips of stone set in the mortar.

Witley

Map 2 ref D7

4 miles S of Godalming on the A283

The historic village of Witley comprises an attractive collection of fine tile-hung and half-timbered buildings loosely arranged around the part-Saxon church of ***All Saints***, a much-altered structure which contains some rare 12th century frescoes and a delicately carved 13th-century font, and incorporates a 17th century tower. The present village inn, the White Hart, was constructed in Elizabethan times to replace an even earlier hostelry. It is believed to be one of the oldest inns in the country and at one time stood adjacent to a marketplace which hosted a busy Friday market.

Witley's ***Old Manor*** was visited by a number English monarchs, including Edward I and Richard II, and the village centre contains some delightful 15th and 16th century timber-framed houses, many of which are hung with characteristic fishtail tiles. These include the Old Cottage, Red Rose Cottage (so-called because the lease granted on Christmas Day 1580 called for an annual rent of one red rose), and Step Cottage, a former rectory which was once the home of Reverend Lawrence Stoughton who died aged 88 after serving the parish for 53 years and outliving five wives.

At one time, Witley was a summer haven for artists and writers, the best known of which is perhaps George Eliot who wrote her last novel, *"Daniel Deronda"*, here between 1874 and 1876. Her home, the Heights, was designed by Sir Henry Cole, the architect of the Royal Albert Hall, and was visited by a series of eminent guests, including the novelist Henry James. Today, the building has been converted into a nursing home and is now known as ***Roslyn Court***.

A large proportion of the common to the north of Thursley is a designated nature reserve which is known for its unusually large and varied population of dragonflies. The ***Witley Common Information Centre*** lies a few minutes' drive from Thursley Common on the eastern side of the A3. This purpose-built nature centre is managed by the National Trust and is set in woodlands at the edge of a substantial area of Trust-owned heathland. Inside, there is an audio-visual display and an exhibition outlining the history, geology and natural history of the area.

Tigburne Court, which is regarded by many as Lutyens's finest work, is just over a mile south of Witley, standing right on the main Milford to Petworth road. It was built in 1899-1901 for Sir Edgar

Tigbourne Court

Horne. Lutyens was 30 years old when he designed Tigburne Court, and the house shows him at the height of his powers yet still full of youthful exuberance. He playfully mixed Tudor styles with 18th century classicism and mixed horizontal bands of tiles with the Bargate stone to create a powerful geometric effect. The gardens, like those of so many of the best Lutyens houses, are by Gertrude Jekyll.

Hambledon *Map 2 ref D8*

5 miles S of Godalming on the A283

This scattered settlement contains a number of interesting buildings, including the tile-hung Court Farm, which stands near the part 14th century church, the Old Granary, School Cottage, and Malthouse Farm and Cottage. The National Trust own a small timber-framed dwelling in Hambledon known as ***Oakhurst Cottage*** which has been restored as an old artisan's home. Open by appointment only.

A memorial to one of the Trust's founders, the social reformer Octavia Hill, stands at the top of nearby ***Hydon's Ball***, an unusual conical hill which at 593 feet above sea level, offers some fine views over the surrounding landscape.

Haslemere *Map 2 ref C9*

9 miles S of Godalming on the A286

The genteel town of Haslemere lies in the southwestern corner of the county. Now a quiet and comfortable home for well-to-do commuters, it has central streets filled with handsome Georgian and Victorian buildings, most of which were constructed following the arrival of the railway in 1859. The building styles, including stucco, redbrick and tile-hung, combine to form an attractive and harmonious architectural mix. Some of Haslemere's finest pre-Victorian structures include the ***Town Hall***, rebuilt in 1814, the ***Tolle House Almshouses*** in Petworth Road, Church Hill House, the Town House, and two noteworthy hotels, the Georgian and the White Horse.

Towards the end of the last century, Haslemere became something of a centre for the arts. Alfred Lord Tennyson settled nearby, and a group known as the Haslemere Society of Artists was formed whose number included Birket Foster and the landscape painter, Helen Allingham. At the end of the First World War, the French-born musician and enthusiastic exponent of early music, Arnold Dolmetsch, founded what has become a world-famous ***musical instrument workshop*** here. Present-day visitors can make an appointment to view the intricately handcrafted harpsichords, lutes and other authentic early instruments being made. Dolmetsch's family went on to establish the Haslemere Festival of Early Music in 1925 which is still held each year in July.

Another of Haslemere's attractions is the ***Educational Museum*** in the High Street, an establishment which was founded in 1888 by local surgeon and Quaker, Sir James Hutchinson, and which now contains an imaginative series of displays on local birds, botany, zoology, geology and history.

Chiddingfold *Map 2 ref D8*

6 miles S of Godalming on the A283

With its three-sided green, waterlily-filled pond, part 13th century church, mediaeval pub and handsome collection of Georgian cottages, this attractive settlement contains all the features of a quintessential English village. During the 13th and 14th centuries, it was an important centre of the glass-making industry, a once flourishing trade which utilised local sand as its main ingredient, timber for fuel, and employed skilled craftspeople from across northern Europe. Some fragments of medieval Chiddingfold glass can be seen in the small lancet window in ***St Mary's Church***, below which a brass plaque can be seen which is inscribed with the names of several early glass-makers. The church itself was much altered during the 1860s; however, its west tower is 17th century and contains a peal of eight bells, one of which is believed to be around 500 years old. The churchyard is entered through an exceptionally fine lych gate, a covered gateway with a wide timber slab which was used to shelter coffins awaiting burial.

Of the many handsome buildings standing around Chiddingfold's village green, the Crown Inn is perhaps the most impressive. This is another hostelry which claims to be the oldest in England, its existence having first been recorded in 1383. The structure is half-timbered and incorporates a medieval great hall; Edward VI is reported to have stayed here in the 15th century. Other buildings in the village worthy of note are Chantry House, Manor House, and Glebe House, the last two of which have elegant Georgian facades.

An 18th century facade is all that remains of ***Shillinglee Park***, a once imposing country mansion which stood in the village until the end of the Second World War. The remainder of the house was destroyed, not by enemy action, but by a party of Canadian service personnel who accidentally set the building on fire during a party to celebrate the allied victory.

Located just south of Chiddingfold on the Guildford to Petworth

Road (the A283) is ***The Ram's Nest Inn***, an attractive free house which makes an ideal reason to stop in this rolling, wooded countryside. The pub was built in 1796 from the proceeds of a robbery. The thieves were later hanged but the pub has continued to flourish. Hanging baskets decorate the glass-roofed veranda at the front of

The Ram's Nest Inn

the pub and the interior is homely and welcoming. The comfortable easy chairs in the bar make ideal vantage points for admiring the wood panelling and the inglenook fireplace. The Inn serves a good range of beers, wines and real ales and the food menu tempts customers to sample baked green-lipped mussels, smoked chicken in a brandy sauce and chicken liver and green peppercorn pate - and these are just the starters. There are twin-bedded guest rooms en-suite upstairs for those who are unwilling to leave at closing time.
The Ram's Nest Inn, Petworth Road, Chiddingfold, Surrey GU8 4SS
Tel: 01428 644460

Dunsfold

Map 2 ref D8

6 miles S of Godalming on the B2130

From Chiddingfold, a pleasant journey eastwards through the country lanes leads to another settlement with fold, (a Saxon term meaning *"forest clearing"*), in its name. Dunsfold is a narrow ribbon of a village which lies on either side a long unmanicured green. It contains a number of fine old brick and tile-hung cottages and houses, several of which date from the late 17th century, and an excellent pub, the Sun Inn which stands beside a towering oak tree which is said to have a girth of over 20 feet.

Dunsfold's finest feature, however, is situated half a mile from the village on top of a raised mound which may once have been the site of a pre-Christian place of worship.

The church of ***St Mary and All Saints*** dates from around 1280 and apart from the addition of a 15th century belfry, has remained virtually unchanged since. The structure was much admired by William Morris, the Victorian founder of the Arts and Crafts Movement, who particularly approved of the simple, rough-hewn pews which were built around 1300 by the inhabitants of the surrounding farms. A leafy glade at the foot of the mound is the location of a holy well whose water is reputed to be a cure for eye complaints and blindness. The site of the well is marked by a timber shelter which was erected in the 1930s.

To the east of Dunsfold, sections of a disused canal can be made out which was built to connect the basins of the Rivers Wey and Arun.

Alfold — *Map 2 ref D9*

9 miles S of Godalming on the B2133

A former clearing in the Wealden forest, Alfold, is an exceptionally attractive village which was once an important glass-making centre. It reputedly supplied material for the windows of Westminster Abbey. Evidence of the medieval glassworks can still be made out in the woods on the edge of the village. The area around the church contains a number of interesting historic features, including an ancient yew tree in the churchyard, a charming Tudor cottage, and an old village whipping post and set of stocks.

Just at the edge of the village is the ***Countryways Experience***, a series of interactive exhibits that covers the history and natural history of this area, giving visitors some perspective on how living conditions adapted to new styles of farming over the centuries.

Ellen's Green — *Map 3 ref F8*

9 miles SE of Godalming on the B2128

This tiny hamlet on the Sussex border is one of the best preserved Surrey villages. It is set in unspoilt Weald country, with thick woodlands giving way to small fields. Cottages line the green but in a way that has no suggestion of excessive self-consciousness. Although singularly lacking in dramatic sights, Ellen's Green offers the visitor the chance to see the sort of small villages that were once was typical of the area but are now in short supply.

Cranleigh
Map 3 ref E8

7 miles SE of Godalming on the B2128

The parish church, St Nicholas, in the quiet residential town of Cranleigh contains a carving of a grinning feline which allegedly provided the inspiration for Lewis Carroll's Cheshire Cat. The town also contains the country's first cottage hospital, opened in the 1850s, and a public school which was founded by local farmers and still incorporates a working farm.

Ewhurst
Map 3 ref F7

8 miles SE of Godalming on the B2127

Ewhurst is a long village containing a sandstone church, ***St Peter and St Paul***, whose nave and south door are considered to be amongst the finest examples of Norman church architecture in the county. The rest of the structure would have been of a similar age had it not been for an unfortunate attempt to underpin the tower in the 1830s which resulted in the collapse, not only of the tower, but of the chancel and north transept as well. The structure was eventually rebuilt in "Norman style" with an unusual shingled broach spire. Inside, there is a carved 14th century font and a Jacobean pulpit, and outside, the churchyard contains a number of mature trees native to North America.

South Doorway, Ewhurst Church

The remainder of the village, part of which is set around a small square, contains some fine 18th and 19th century residential buildings, including the ***Woolpit***, built for the Doulton family in the 1880s. The 843 foot ***Pitch Hill*** is situated a mile to the north and can be easily reached along a pleasant footpath from the village.

Yard Farm, owned by Nick and Moira Nutting, lives up to its own description as 'a peaceful haven'. Horses roam the 400 acres of farmland, nestled near the village of Ewhurst in a fold of the Surrey countryside, and the Nuttings offer bed and breakfast on their charming working farm. The farmhouse itself dates from the sixteenth century and features fine old exterior beams as well as original fittings - including an Elizabethan wig cupboard - in the bedrooms and guests' sitting room. Yard Farm makes an ideal base for rambling on the nearby North Downs, bird-watching or simply relaxing

Yard Farm

in the heated pool back at the farm. Ewhurst, the nearest village, has a mill that was formerly used by smugglers as a hiding place for their contraband. The Nuttings also offer a special airport service, allowing guests an overnight stay, delivery to Gatwick and car parking while they are out of the country. *Yard Farm, Ewhurst, Cranleigh, Surrey GU6 7SN Tel: 01483 276649*

CHAPTER SIX
Around Dorking

Sutton Abinger

Chapter 6 - Area Covered

For precise location of places please refer to the colour maps found at the rear of the book.

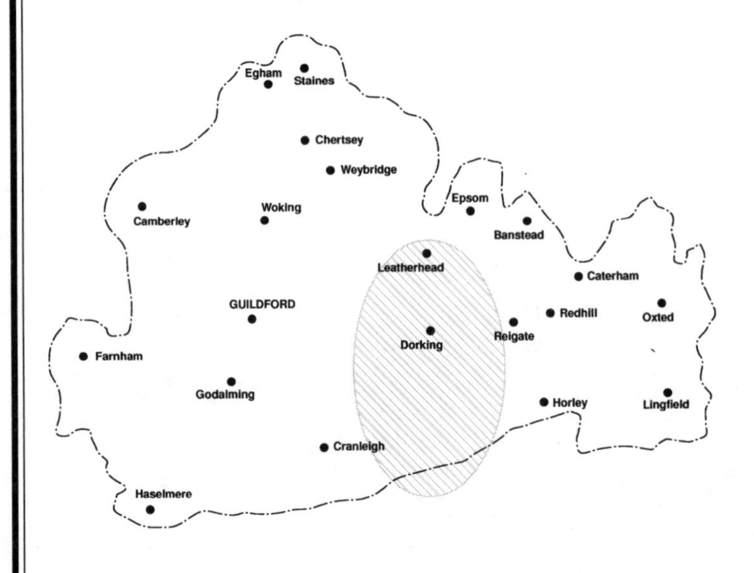

6
Around Dorking

Introduction

Dorking lies at the centre of an oblong that stretches from Leatherhead and the M25 in the north southwards to the Surrey border near Gatwick Airport. It is remarkable that although this area is defined by two of the largest man-made additions to the landscape, the land lying between them should be so spared from a headlong rush to development.

With the exception of Dorking and Leatherhead, there are no towns of significant size in the area covered in the following pages. On the contrary; there are small towns, wayside villages, and scattered homesteads that could only be described as hamlets with a considerable degree of exaggeration.

This is the geographical heart of Surrey and it contains most of the landscapes that are associated with the county. The two major towns have their suburban tracts, but there are also sweeping swathes of open farmland mingling with copses and larger woodlands. The highest point in the Southeast of England, Leith Hill, is within shouting distance of Dorking, and the wooded slopes near the Sussex border have led to the nickname *"Little Switzerland"*. Indeed it is in that southern stretch of land, high up overlooking the Weald, that a sense of real remoteness - lost almost everywhere else in the Southeast - can be felt.

Dorking

Dorking is a long-established settlement which stands at the intersection of Stane Street, the Roman road which once connected London with Chichester, and the ancient Pilgrims' Way east-west ridgeway route which is roughly followed by the course of the modern North Downs Way. Despite evidence of Saxon and Viking occupation, present-day Dorking is a congested commuter town which owes most of its character to the Victorians.

There are a small number of older buildings, most notably the part 15th century former coaching inn, the White Horse, and the shops and houses in North Street, West Street, and at the western end of the High Street; however, the town's two most distinctive architectural features are characteristically 19th century: the unexpectedly grand parish church of ***St Martin*** with its soaring spire, and the ***Rose Hill*** housing development, an assortment of Victorian villas arranged around a green and entered from South Street through an unusual neo-Gothic arch. St Paul's Church in Dorking is a fine piece of architecture, designed by Benjamin Ferray and constructed in 1857.

Perhaps Dorking's most attractive feature is its close proximity to unspoilt countryside, a testimony to the success of the South East's Green Belt policy. As well as the open spaces in the downs to the north, ***Holmwood Common***, 2 miles along the A24 to the south, is another tract of National Trust-owned land which offers some pleasant waymarked walks through mature oak and birch woodlands.

West Street in Dorking has some fine old buildings, few of which predate the premises of ***Partners & Sons Restaurant***. This highly regarded eating establishment occupies numbers 2, 3, and 4 West Street and its oldest part (formerly numbers 3 and 4) were built in 1563. Number 4 is the "newcomer", with its 1612 vintage; the two properties were merged as recently as 1990 when the original Partners Restaurant was founded. The present proprietor, Irmgard Bland, took over in March 1997, when the restaurant was refurbished and given its present look, which adds a note of modern brightness without trampling on the building's rich history.

Open every day except Tuesday for lunch and dinner, Partners and Sons also manages a neat blend in its menu, which specialises in a deft combination of English and Mediterranean cuisine. This means that a hearty Angus steak can follow a risotto of deep-fried prosciutto with sweet and sour peppers. Luscious puddings and an

Partners & Sons Restaurant

extensive wine list complete this memorable dining experience. *Partners and Sons, 2/4 West Street, Dorking, Surrey RH4 1BL Tel: 01306 882826*

North of Dorking

Ranmore Common — *Map 3 ref G6*

1 mile NW of Dorking off the A2003

As its name suggests, Ranmore Common benefits from open space, and its location on the top of the Downs provides some excellent views, especially looking south. This unspoilt setting, which can feel remote in bad weather and yet is so close to Dorking, is a testament to enlightened Green Belt policy. The common is in reality a long green, with only a few houses dotted around it, thereby preserving the exposed nature of this expanse.

Dunley Hill Farm, with its spacious fields and well-established trees, provides a lovely setting for ***The Old Cartlodge Tea Rooms***, which stretch along a low-slung pantiled building at the end of a handsome drive in Ranmore Common, near Dorking. Owner Mary

The Old Cartlodge Tearooms

Suckling and her staff have devoted their energies into providing a wide range of refreshments and farm merchandise in these welcoming surroundings. Hanging baskets and horse troughs cascade with flowers outside, while flowering shrubs hug the walls by the large gravel car park. The handsome red-brick cartlodge provides an appropriately rural welcome for the walkers, bird-watchers and general nature lovers who flock to the Ranmore Common, which is acknowledged as one of Surrey's beauty spots. Look for the sign that reads *'Hikers take your boots off before entering this abode'.* Many of the customers are repeat visitors and it is worth phoning ahead to book a table. Easy wheelchair access means that the Old Cartlodge can extend a special welcome to disabled visitors. *The Old Cartlodge Tea Rooms, Dunley Hill Farm, Ranmore Common, near Dorking, Surrey Tel: 01483 282222*

Westcott

Map 3 ref F6

2 miles W of Dorking on the A25

Westcott is a tidy village that lies on the main road linking Dorking with Shere. Although most of the houses are from the same Victorian period, they display a variety of building styles. This diversity stems from the fact that Westcott lies almost exactly at the junction of the chalk North Downs and the sandstone Surrey Hills. Both of these stone types figure in the design of the cottages, and sometimes both are used in the same house. Churtgate House, built in the 16th century, predates nearly all the other buildings in Westcott; it is located on the main road at the corner of Balchin's Lane.

East Clandon — *Map 3 ref E5*

7 miles W of Dorking on the A246

Forming a settlement straddling the A246 Leatherhead to Guildford route is this attractive small village. The road zig-zags between brick and half-timber cottages, several of which are clustered around the Norman church of St Thomas. This small church was extensively restored at the end of the 19th century but the architects ensured that one of is most distinctive features - the bulky shingled bell tower - retained its original appearance.

The village also contains an interesting old forge and a lovely old manor farmhouse dating from the late 17th century. A striking National Trust property is located 1 mile to the northeast; ***Hatchlands Park*** is a distinctive brick-built house which was designed in the mid 18th century for Admiral Boscawen after his famous victory in the Battle of Louisburg. Inside, there are some splendid examples of the early work of Robert Adams, some fine period furniture and paintings, and a wonderful assortment of historic keyboard instruments, the Cobbe collection, which was moved here in 1988. The grounds were originally laid out by Repton and have since been remodelled by Gertrude Jekyll; in recent years, they have undergone a process of restoration and been opened up to visitors.

East Horsley — *Map 3 ref F5*

6 miles W of Dorking on the A246

Suburban building has caught up with East Horsley, leaving the town centre bereft of the sort of charm associated with Ranmore Common or some of the other villages that are nearer Dorking. It does, however, possess one of the more dramatic country houses in Surrey, at least as it is viewed from the road and its entrance. ***East Horsley Towers***, built in the 1820s, seems to capture the spirit of the 19th century imagination as it moved from Romantic to the nostalgic re-creations so beloved of the Victorians. A long entrance leads to the house, which presents itself with a huge round tower by the entrance. Another tower, to the west, is built in the Gothic style. The house itself displays Tudor influences but has multi-coloured vaulting ribs throughout for support. Another tower, this time Germanic looking with a pointed roof, dominates the east wing of the house.

Effingham — *Map 3 ref F5*

5 miles W of Dorking on the A246

Efffingham is an old village that was famous as the home of the

Howards of Effingham, one of whom was the Commander-in-Chief of the English fleet which defeated the Spanish Armada in 1588. His home was Effingham Court Palace, which survives only as remnants as ***Lower Place Farm***.

There were two other important manors in Effingham. One is the moated grange in Great Lee Wood, once the manor of Effingham la Leigh; the other was the medieval property of the Earls of Gloucester, East Court, which is now incorporated in a boarding school, St Theresa's Convent.

Ockham *Map 3 ref F5*

10 miles NW of Dorking on the B2039

Ockham once possessed a fine Jacobean mansion, Ockham Park. A serious fire in 1948 destroyed everything except for the orangery, stables, kitchen wing, and a solitary Italianate tower. The village church of ***All Saints*** still stands within the grounds of the estate; this largely 13th century building was constructed on the site of a pre-Norman structure and is known for its remarkable east window, a surprising combination of seven tall pointed lancets finished in marble with distinctive carved capitals. The window dates from around 1260 and is thought to have been brought here from nearby Newark Abbey following its dissolution in the 16th century. The church incorporates a brick chapel which contains a robed marble effigy of the first Lord King, the former owner of Ockham Park who died in 1734.

The Hautboy, one of Surrey's most distinctive country hotels, occupies a peaceful setting directly opposite the cricket pitch in the village of Ockham. The building itself dates from the mid nineteenth century, and owner Richard Watney has lovingly preserved all the details incorporated by the famous Victorian architect William, the 1st Earl of Lovelace. Features such as decorative quatre foils and Tudor-style windows on the brick exterior set the stage for the sumptuous interior, with its five charmingly individual suites - including one with a four-poster. There the visitors are pampered with a range of conveniences, typical of a luxury hotel but in keeping with the period feel that permeates the Hautboy.

The hotel has a choice of two restaurants and a cellar bar. The Chapel, originally the Great Hall, has been restored in the style of a Tuscan chapel with spectacular frescoes and hand-built Gothic furniture. It features the cooking of Darren Tidd, formerly senior sous at Cliveden, and offers a stunning range of seasonal dishes. The Oboe provides more informal meals in a relaxed setting with ex-

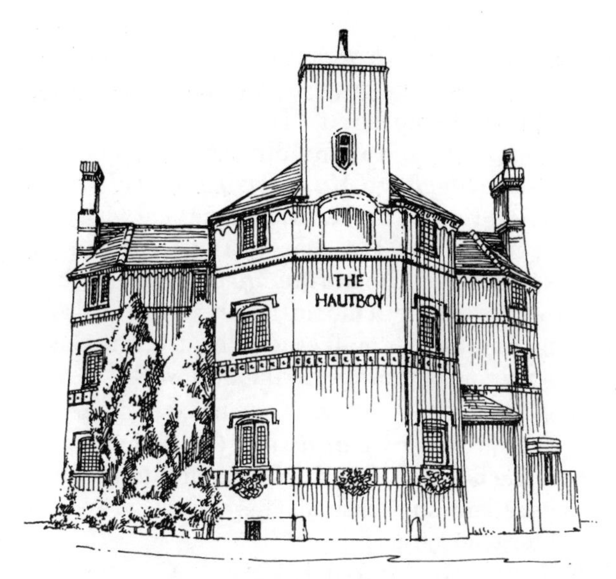

The Hautboy

posed mellow brickwork and oak floors - it also features a tempting mix of modern and traditional dishes. Ockham lies midway between Heathrow and Gatwick airports, so the Hautboy provides an oasis for travellers or anyone seeking a break from the modern world. *The Hautboy, Ockham Lane, Ockham, Surrey GU23 6NP Tel: 01483 225355*

On ***Chatley Heath***, 1 mile to the north of Ockham, there is a unique Semaphore Tower which was once part of the Royal Navy's signalling system for relaying messages between Portsmouth and the Admiralty in London. Although the semaphore mechanism soon fell into disuse, the structure has remained in good order and is open to the public at weekends. As well as offering outstanding views over the surrounding landscape, the ***Chatley Heath Semaphore Tower*** houses an interesting exhibition and model collection. It can be reached along a pleasant woodland pathway and is open on weekends and Bank Holidays.

Leatherhead *Map 3 ref G5*

5 miles N of Dorking on the A24

Leatherhead is a pretty Mole Valley town which manages to retain some measure of tranquillity despite being crossed by a number of major trunk routes. Several buildings in the narrow streets of the old town are worthy of note, including the 16th century Running Horse Inn and the attractive part 12th century parish church of St Mary and St Nicholas. The grave of Anthony Hope (real name Sir Anthony Hawkins), the author of *"The Prisoner Of Zenda"*, can be found in the churchyard, and a short distance away in Church Street, the informative ***Leatherhead Museum of Local History*** is housed in a charming 17th century timber-framed cottage with its own small garden. Built in 1968 in the characteristic style of the period, Leatherhead's celebrated ***Thorndike Theatre*** offers a first-rate programme of drama, dance and music theatre; there is also a pleasant coffee shop and bar, and a small studio theatre, the Casson Room, offering a programme of more experimental work.

Leatherhead is well served with its choice of shops and attractions, but few can match ***Fire and Iron Gallery*** for pure interest. The Gallery is the brainchild of the Quinnell family, who sought to establish an excellent showcase for metalwork, in response to the resurgence of forged iron as a creative medium. Fire and Iron Gallery harks back to Britain's centuries-old tradition of blacksmithing while displaying the best work of contemporary British and overseas metalsmiths. The gallery is located in a Grade II star listed farmhouse which dates back to 1450; there is ample parking just outside.

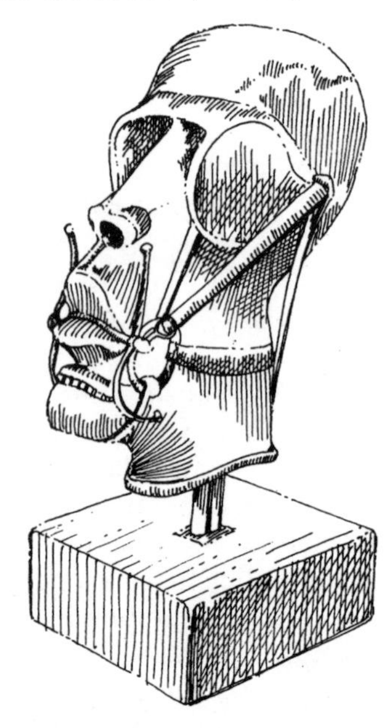

Fire and Iron Gallery

The interior is an eye-catching collection of the full range of metalworking, with delicate jewellery sharing space with exquisite beds and fascinating life-size animal sculptures. Lucy Quinnell, the director, is a charming mine of information about the displays. She can provide advice about rust-proofing and restoration and welcomes commissions for new pieces. The Gallery is open from 10 to 5 and closes only on Sundays and Bank Holidays. *Fire and Iron Gallery, Rowhurst Forge, Leatherhead, Surrey KT22 0EN Tel: 01372 386453*

Great Bookham — *Map 3 ref G5*

4 miles N of Dorking on the A246

Although heavily built up since the Second World War, the residential area to the west of Leatherhead manages to retain something of its historic past. The earliest mention of a settlement in the area dates back to the 660's AD when a manor at Bocheham is recorded as belonging to Chertsey Abbey.

Present-day Great Bookham contains an exceptional parish church, ***St Nicholas***, which has an unusual flint tower with a shingled spire dating back to the Norman era in the 12th century. A substantial part of the building, including the chancel, is known to have been rebuilt in the 1340's by the Abbot of Chertsey, and the church was again remodelled by the Victorians. Inside, there is some fine 15th century stained glass and a number of noteworthy monumental brasses and memorials to the local lords of the manor. An early 18th century owner of the Bookham estate, Dr Hugh Shortrudge, left an endowment in his will to four local churches on condition that an annual sermon was preached on the subject of the martyrdom of Charles I. St Nicholas continues to uphold the tradition of the *"Shortrudge sermon"* which is preached each year on the final Sunday in January.

Nearby ***Little Bookham*** has a small single-roomed church with a wooden belfry which is believed to date from the 12th century. The adjacent 18th century manor house now operates as a school. ***Bookham Common*** and ***Banks Common*** to the northwest of Little Bookham provide some welcome relief from the commuter estates and offer some pleasant walking through relatively unspoilt open heathland. The commons are recorded in the Domesday Book as providing pannage, the right to graze pigs on acorns, for Chertsey Abbey. Now under the ownership of the National Trust, they are particularly known for their rich and varied birdlife.

Another National Trust-owned property, ***Polesden Lacey***, stands on high ground 2 miles to the south of Great Bookham. The estate was once owned by the writer R B Sheridan who purchased it in 1797 with the intention of restoring its decaying 17th century manor house; however, a lack of funds prevented him from realising his ambitions, and following his death in 1816, the building was demolished and the estate sold. Then during the 1820's, the architect Thomas Cubitt built a substantial Regency villa in its place which was subsequently remodelled and enlarged by successive owners throughout the 19th century.

Thatched Bridge, Polesden Lacey

In 1906, the estate was acquired by Captain Ronald Greville and his wife Margaret, the daughter of a Scottish brewing magnate and a celebrated high society hostess. Over the following three decades, they invited a succession of rich and influential guests to Polesden Lacey whose number included Edward VII, and George VI and Queen Elizabeth (now the Queen Mother) who spent part of their honeymoon here in 1923. The Grevilles carried out a number of alterations of their own during this period and the extravagant "Edwardian-Louis XVI" internal decoration remains as a testimony to Margaret Greville's taste (or, some may say, the lack of it).

Whatever the perspective, the house contains an undeniably fine collection of furniture, paintings, tapestries, porcelain and silver which the Grevilles accumulated over 40 years, and Margaret's personal collection of photographs provides a fascinating record of British high society at play during the early part of the century. The surrounding grounds amount to over 1,000 acres and incorporate a walled rose garden, open lawns, a YHA youth hostel and a large area of natural woodland; there is also a charming open-air theatre which holds an annual season of events in late-June and early-July.

The Polesden Lacey estate is bordered to the south by ***Ranmore Common***, another area of National Trust-owned upland which is criss-crossed by scenic footpaths and bridleways. This scenic area of the North Downs provides some good walking, and also offers a couple of excellent places to restore oneself afterwards, and there is a super tea room at Dunley Hill Farm.

Mickleham *Map 3 ref G5*

3 miles N of Dorking on the A24

Mickleham is a highly picturesque village with a good pub, the Running Horses, and a restored Norman church, ***St Michael***, containing a rare Flemish stained-glass window. It is worth examining the churchyard because this is one of the few parish churches to preserve the Surrey tradition of grave-boards. These are wooden tombstone planks which are carried between two posts. Most of the grave-boards in St Michael's are 19th century although they have been carefully preserved and renovated where necessary.

A little further afield, pleasant open countryside can also be found on ***Mickleham Down*** (part of which is known locally as Little Switzerland)

The Old London Road, which runs through the pretty village of Mickleham, is the setting for ***The Running Horses***, a wayside pub that has attracted thirsty travellers for more than 400 years. One can easily imagine the road a few hundred years ago, thronged with peddlers and merchants, coachmen and dandies. Such a cross-section of society must have been tempting for highwaymen, and the main bar of the running Horses features a highwayman's hideaway. Today's customers are a more peaceable lot, preferring to stay put by the cheerful blazes in the inglenook fireplaces, sipping a pint while they peruse the extensive menu.

The Running Horses

This is where the Running Horses really comes into its own, with fortifying choices ranging from fresh mussels and crusty bread and hot wild boar sausage baguettes to hearty imaginative main courses - a particular favourite is pork fillet stuffed with prunes wrapped in bacon. Steve and Josie Slayford are welcoming hosts and can tell you about the origins of the pub name, which commemorates the famous dead heat in the 1828 Derby. *The Running Horses, Old London Road, Mickleham, Surrey RH5 6DU Tel: 01372 372279, Fax: 01372 363004*

Boxhill — *Map 3 ref G5*

2 miles N of Dorking off the A25

The 563 foot Box Hill lies a couple of miles from Polesden Lacey on the eastern side of the River Mole. This popular local landmark rises sharply from the valley floor to an impressive tree-covered summit, 400 feet above. The hill takes its name from the mature box trees which once grew here in profusion but which were seriously depleted in the 18th century to supply the needs of London wood-engravers. By then, the site had already been known for over a century as a beauty spot and had been visited by, among others, the diarist John Evelyn.

Today, the National Trust owns over 800 acres of land around Box Hill which has now been designated a country park. The area around the summit incorporates an exhibition centre, a late 19th century fort and a take-away cafe, and can be reached either by footpath or by a narrow winding road which leads up from Burford Bridge. The hillside is traversed by a series of nature walks, and there are also several picnic sites which enjoy breathtaking views across the Weald to the South Downs.

The Burford Bridge Hotel stands on the banks of the River Mole at the foot of Box Hill and is connected to it by stepping stones across the river. In the early 19th century, the establishment was known as the Hare and Hounds and it was here that in 1805, Admiral Nelson said his farewells to Lady Hamilton prior to the Battle of Trafalgar; Keats is also believed to have completed his second volume of poems *"Endymion"* here in 1818. Chapel Farm at nearby West Humble is an open farm which offers visitors the chance to see a working livestock farm at close quarters.

Brockham — *Map 3 ref G6*

1 miles N of Dorking on the A25

Brockham is a picture-postcard village set around a quintessential three-sided village green on which cricket is played in summer, a

Guy Fawkes' bonfire is lit in autumn, and Christmas carols are sung in winter. The legendary cricketer W G Grace is even said to have played here. This delightful tree-lined setting is enhanced by a splendid view of Box Hill, some fine old cottages, and an elegantly proportioned parish church with a tall spire which was built in the 1840s in uncomplicated Early English style. Other noteworthy buildings in the village include the late 18th century ***Brockham Court***, which can be seen on the eastern edge of the green, and the part 17th century Feltons Farm, which lies a short distance away to the southwest. The remains of some 19th century industrial kilns can be seen on the Downs above the village in the disused ***Brockham Quarries***.

South of Dorking

Abinger *Map 3 ref F6*

4 miles SW of Dorking off the A25

The parish of Abinger contains two villages, Abinger itself (or ***Abinger Common***) which lies one mile west of Friday Street at the southern end of the parish, and ***Abinger Hammer*** which lies on the A25 Dorking to Guildford road to the north. Abinger claims to be one of the oldest settlements in the country, having been settled by Middle Stone Age people around 5000 BC. The remains of a Mesolithic pit-dwelling were discovered in a field near Abinger's old ***Manor House*** which, when excavated in 1950, revealed over 1,000 tools and artefacts which are now on display in an interesting little museum.

Abinger's parish church of ***St James*** is an unlucky building. This part 12th century structure was largely destroyed by an enemy flying bomb during World War II. It was rebuilt, with great sensitivity, but was severely damaged in 1964 after being struck by lightning. In the churchyard there is a war memorial designed by Lutyens, and in the corner of the three-side village green, a set of old wooden stocks and a whipping post.

Abinger Common is a delightful hamlet that lies one and a half miles north of Leith Hill, the birthplace of the first Archbishop of Canterbury whose name lives on in the title of an enchanting pub, ***The Stephen Langton Inn***. This inn, with its attractive beamed exterior, has a lovely location next to a small pond. The beams are much in evidence inside as well, glowing warmly in the light of the blazing log fire. Run by a popular brother and sister team, Jan and

The Stephen Langton Inn

Maria, the Stephen Langton Inn matches its traditional beverages with a good selection of hearty and imaginative menu choices. Tried and tested pub favourites are always available but it's worth trying the dish of the day, which might even be Mexican. The surrounding countryside, which is the highest in Surrey, is still heavily wooded, and the pub benefits from a steady flow of walkers and riders who pass along the adjacent trails. *The Stephen Langton Inn, Friday Street, Abinger Common, near Dorking, Surrey RH5 6JR Tel: 01306 730775*

Abinger Hammer, just over a mile to the northwest, lies in the valley of the River Tillingbourne, a fast-flowing stream which in the 15th and 16th centuries was used to power the mechanical metal-working hammers from which the settlement takes its name. At one time, the village was known for the manufacture of cannon balls and a busy blacksmith's workshop can still be found here. Abinger Hammer's industrial past is reflected in the famous "Jack the Smith" hammer clock which was erected in 1909. This unique clock overhangs the road on the site of an old iron forge and is characterised by the figure of a blacksmith who strikes a bell with his hammer every half hour.

It would be hard to locate the hamlet of Sutton Abinger on even the most detailed map - a clue is that it is near Dorking - but if you do find it, you must stop at ***The Volunteer***. You would be hard pressed to find a more unspoilt pub in such rural surroundings anywhere in Surrey, or indeed anywhere in the county. It abuts the corner of a small road and an even smaller lane, and has presented

The Volunteer

its handsome whitewashed appearance to wayfarers for centuries. The ideal way to arrive would be on horseback, with news of Wellington's victory or Victoria's accession to the throne, but today's customers can make do with the ample car park to the side. The interior is equally redolent of the past, with blazing fire and old timbers providing a backdrop for the good choice of food and drink. You can complete the experience by asking manager Naomi Davidson if one of the two guest rooms are available for bed and breakfast. *The Volunteer, Water Lane, Sutton Abinger, near Dorking, Surrey RH5 6PR Tel: 01306 730798*

Sutton Abinger

Holmbury St Mary
Map 3 ref F7

6 miles W of Dorking on the B2126

Holmbury St Mary was the invention of well-to-do Victorians, one of whom, George Edmund Street, designed and paid for the church in 1879. The village provides a good access point to the 857 foot Holmbury Hill, an upland with an altogether wilder feel than Leith Hill, its taller neighbour across the valley. A pleasant walk leads to the remains of an 8 acre Iron Age hill fort whose fading earthwork fortifications lie hidden amongst the undergrowth on the hillside.

Leith Hill
Map 3 ref G7

5 miles SW of Dorking on the B2126

The 965 foot National Trust-owned Leith Hill is the highest point in the southeast of England. In 1766, a 64 foot tower was built on the tree-covered summit by Richard Hull, a local squire who lived at nearby Leith Hill Place; he now lies buried beneath his splendid creation. Present-day visitors climbing to the top on a clear day can enjoy a panorama which takes in several counties and reaches as far as the English Channel.

The part 17th, part 18th century ***Leith Hill Place*** stands within beautiful rhododendron filled grounds which are open to public on a limited number of days each year. In its time, the house has been owned by the Wedgwood and Vaughan Williams families, and inside, there is a fine collection of Wedgwood pottery and paintings by such artists as Reynolds and Stubbs. An Edwardian country house designed by Sir Edwin Lutyens can be found on the northern slopes of Leith Hill; Goddards on Abinger Common stands within attractive grounds laid out by Gertrude Jekyll and was first opened to visitors in the spring of 1992.

Coldharbour
Map 3 ref G7

5 miles SW of Dorking off the A29

A remote hamlet set 700 feet up in the Surrey Hills, Coldharbour has an atmosphere that is light-years away from most people's preconception of surrey as a county of cosy suburbs and smiling farmland. Sturdy, stone-built houses cling to the hilltop, from which there are magnificent views sweeping south over the Weald.

Just to the north of Coldharbour is ***Anstiebury Camp***, an Iron Age fort that was probably built in the 1st or 2nd century BC. The fort is oval in plan, covering more than 11 acres and is defended by triple banks with double ditches to the north and northeast.

Ockley *Map 3 ref G7*

8 miles SW of Dorking on the A29

At Ockley there is a village green which, at over 500 feet in diameter, is one of the largest in Surrey. In summer, village cricket is played in this classic English setting which is enhanced by a number of handsome period houses and cottages. Ockley has had a long and eventful history: the village once stood on ***Stane Street***, the old Roman road between Chichester and London which is now partially followed by the route of the A29, and in the mid 9th century, a momentous battle between the forces of King Ethelwulf of the West Saxons and the marauding Vikings reputedly took place near here. Following the Norman invasion, the surrounding woodlands were designated a royal hunting forest and in the 12th century, the Normans built a fortification half-a-mile to the north of the present village green which has long since disappeared. However, the nearby part 14th century church of St Margaret remains, although this was extensively remodelled by the Victorians during the 1870s.

Among the many other noteworthy buildings in Ockley are the 18th century ***Ockley Court***, which stands opposite the church, and the groups of cottages surrounding the green which are built in a variety of styles and materials, including brick, tiling and weatherboarding. An interesting private sculpture and ceramics gallery, the ***Hannah Peschar Gallery-Garden***, which incorporates a delightful water garden can be found in Standon Lane.

A short distance to the southwest of Ockley, a chapel was built in the 13th century to serve the population of this once-isolated part of the Weald. Known as the Okewood Chapel, it was later endowed by a local nobleman after his son narrowly avoided being savaged by a wild boar when a mystery arrow struck and killed the charging animal.

Newdigate *Map 3 ref G7*

5 miles S of Dorking off the A24

A turning east off the A24 at Beare Green leads to the village of Newdigate. This historic settlement contains an interesting parish church, ***St Peter's***, which is believed to have been founded in the 12th century by the Earl de Warenne as a *"hunters' chapel"*, a place of worship built to be used by Norman hunting parties during their expeditions in the Wealden forest. The tower, with its shingled spire, was constructed around a massive cross-braced timber frame in the 15th century, a time when Newdigate was relatively prosperous thanks to its flourishing iron-founding industry. The oak shingles on the spire had to be replaced in the late 1970's after their Victorian predecessors had warped in the hot summer of 1976.

Present-day Newdigate contains a number of exceptional old timber-framed buildings, several of which date back to the 16th century and before.

Charlwood *Map 3 ref H7*

8 miles S of Dorking off the A24

A charming period village on the Sussex border, Charlwood is all the more admirable in that it is so near Crawley and Gatwick Airport and yet preserves so much of its own rural identity. Although it lacks the sense of remoteness which it must once have possessed - and which only rarely survives in villages such as Coldharbour - Charlwood still has many 18th century cottages and a sprinkling of earlier, slightly larger yeomen's houses such as the 15th century ***Charlwood House*** to the southeast of the village centre.

The parish ***Church of St Nicholas*** was built in the 11th century and underwent a series of alterations, extensions and renovations beginning in the 13th century. The impression, surprisingly, is

Medieval Screen, Charlwood Church

one of an organic building that has evolved with the centuries. One of its prized possessions is the late medieval screen, one of the most intricately carved pieces of ecclesiastical woodwork in Surrey.

CHAPTER SEVEN
Southeast Surrey

Lingfield Church Monument

Chapter 7 - Area Covered

For precise location of places please refer to the colour maps found at the rear of the book.

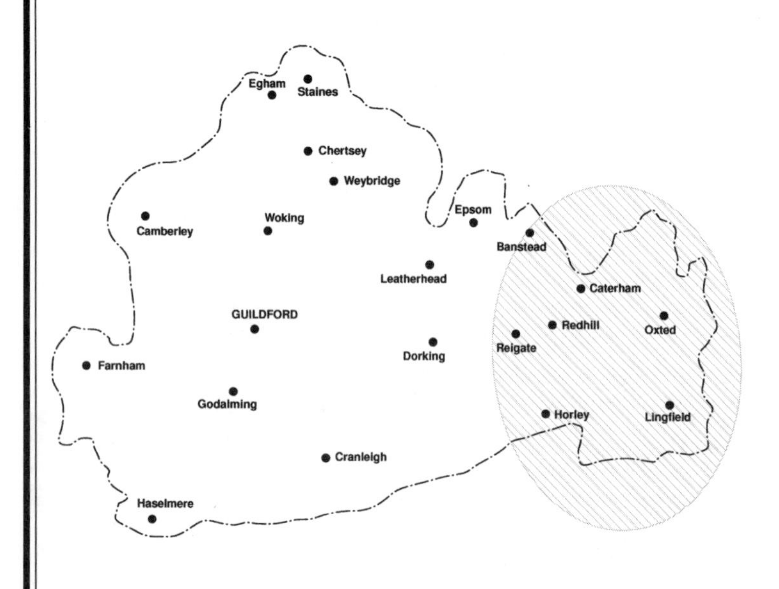

7
Southeast Surrey

Introduction

The southeast corner of Surrey abuts both Kent to the east and Sussex to the south. Not surprisingly there are elements of both counties in some of the Surrey border villages, noticeable in particular in the way that Kent weatherboarding features in the villages and hamlets near Lingfield.

The M25 marks the northern extremity of the area covered in this chapter. As with so many other parts of the county, the towns and villages lying just south of the motorway have fought - and largely won - a battle to preserve their sense of identity. Perhaps it is simply because they have had many centuries to grow accustomed to east-west traffic. The valleys and ridges here comprised the route followed by religious devotees on their way from London and further afield to Canterbury. Indeed many stretches of the original Pilgrims' Way, which is now well-marked trail along much of its route, look down on its modern, secular, counterpart, the M25.

The countryside in this southeastern corner is far less wooded than south-central or southwestern Surrey. Instead it is a land of open fields and church spires spotted on the horizon. Only at the southern edge, where it nears the Weald of Kent, does the landscape begin to become defined by its woodlands.

Reigate

Reigate is a prosperous residential town whose expansion at the hands of postwar developers has done much to conceal its long and distinguished history. The settlement was once an important outpost of the de Warenne family, the assertive Norman rulers whose sphere of influence stretched from the Channel coast to the North Downs. As at Lewes, they built a castle on a rise above the village streets of which nothing remains today except for an arch which was reconstructed in the 1770s from material recovered from the original castle walls. Today, this striking neo-Gothic reproduction stands at the heart of a pleasant public park.

A steep path leads down from the castle mound to the attractive mixture of Victorian, Georgian and older buildings which line Reigate's High Street. The ***Old Town Hall***, a handsome redbrick building constructed in 1729, stands at its eastern end, and a short distance away to the north, the entrance to a disused road tunnel can be seen which was built beneath the castle mound in 1824 to ease the through-flow of traffic on the busy London to Brighton coaching route. Other noteworthy buildings in this part of town include the timber-framed and tile-fronted ***"La Trobes"*** in the High Street, and the 400 year old ***Old Sweep's House*** in the charmingly named Slipshoe Street.

As well as being effective administrators, the de Warennes were known for their devout religious beliefs, and again as at Lewes, they founded a priory in the town some distance from the centre. After the Dissolution, this became the home of Lord Howard of Effingham, the commander-in-chief of the English navy at the time of the Spanish Armada. The building has been remodelled on a number of occasions since then, in particular during the Georgian era, and now operates as a school. The interior contains some fine period features and an interesting museum. Also set away from the town centre, and probably standing on the site of pre-Norman Reigate, is the pale stone-built church of ***St Mary Magdalene***. This con-

Monument to Rebecca Waterlow
St Mary Magdalene

tains a number of striking memorials, including one carved by Joseph Rose the Elder around 1730.

Unbelievable, but true - ***The Skimmington Castle*** is a genuine, hideaway pub that was once a highwayman's haunt and yet is only a short drive from Reigate town centre. This lovely old pub is located on Reigate Heath on the edge of its picturesque golf course and surrounded by period houses and beautiful countryside. The interior of the pub is a real Aladdin's cave and includes an amazing collection of keys as well as brassware, farm implements and other rustic items, all set around a magnificent inglenook fireplace. Once

The Skimmington Castle

you've found the "Skim" your thirst will be quenched from a selection of real ales and wine by the glass. Best of all is an extensive range of freshly prepared meals to suit any occasion and everyone's taste, from light snacks to a full three-course meal, including plenty of fresh fish, fine cuts of meat and traditional home-made puddings. The Skimmington Castle certainly merits its reputation for excellent food and is well worth the search - you won't be disappointed. *The Skimmington Castle, Bonny's Road, Reigate Heath, Reigate, Surrey RH2 8RL Tel: 01737 243100*

Around Reigate

Redhill — *Map 4 ref I6*

2 miles E of Reigate on the A23

Redhill developed around the railway station after the London to Brighton line opened in the 1840s. The new rail line ran parallel to the corresponding road (now the A23) and cut through previously open landscape. Most of Redhill's buildings consequently date from that period or the decades shortly afterwards. The parish church of St John has an exceptionally tall and elegant spire, and the ***Harlequin Theatre*** in the Warwick Quadrant shopping precinct offers a full programme of drama, film and musical entertainment in addition to having a pleasant bar, restaurant, and coffee shop.

Buckland *Map 4 ref H6*

3 miles W of Reigate on the A25

Buckland is a pretty settlement which suffers from being sited on the busy main road. The road divides Buckland's tidy rectangular green from the parish church of St Mary, a part 13th century structure whose interior is worth a look for its 15th century stained-glass east window and 17th century pews and oak panelling. The A25 to the east of Buckland passes along the northern edge of ***Reigate Heath***; this narrow area of open heathland is the home of the unique ***Windmill Church***, the only church in the world to be situated in a windmill.

Betchworth *Map 4 ref H6*

3 miles W of Reigate off the A25

Betchworth was once a much more important settlement than it is today. In the 14th century, it had its own fortress, Betchworth Castle, which stood beside the River Mole on a site now occupied by the local golf course. This has now virtually disappeared and the only reminder of Betchworth's past glory is the parish church of ***St Michael***, a surprisingly imposing structure which incorporates some ancient Saxon masonry, a Norman arch and a succession of more recent architectural modifications. Inside, there is a fascinating map of the local manor dated 1634 showing the vestiges of the feudal field system and a wooden chest which is reputed to have been made before the Norman invasion from a single piece of timber taken from a 1,000 year old oak tree; there is also an unusual font dating from the 1950's. The church is situated at the end of a wide cul-de-sac which also contains an early 18th century vicarage, an old long barn, and a collection of attractive 17th and 18th century cottages.

A number of interesting buildings can be seen in other parts of Betchworth, including the 16th century Old Mill Cottage, the slender Queen Anne "Old House", and Betchworth House, an impressive part-Georgian manor house which is surrounded by pretty parkland.

Leigh

Map 4 ref H6

4 miles S of Reigate of the A217

Leigh (pronounced lye) is a well-kept village which, like at least a dozen others in Britain, takes its name from the Saxon term for forest clearing.

Located right in the middle of the village of Leigh is ***The Plough***, a popular local pub that has been providing a welcome for centuries. The building itself, with its red tile and white clapboard exterior, is a listed building and parts of it date back to the 15th century. The interesting combination of building styles, proof of its centuries-old pedigree, leads to an equally pleasing medley of pub areas.

The Plough

There is a locals bar as well as a separate and cosy lounge bar. The separate restaurant area overlooks the garden and the village green. Real ales and well-kept wines help to slake thirsts and owner Sarah Bloomfield ensures that there is always a varied selection of bar snacks as well as full-scale meals available. The Plough wears its age well without being a stuffy time capsule - special evenings such as the arrival of Beaujolais Nouveau (with an all French menu) and the Australia Day quiz keep the atmosphere lively. *Tne Plough, Church Road, Leigh, Surrey RH2 8NJ Tel 01306 611348*

Like Newdigate and Charlwood to the south, Leigh was an important centre of the Wealden iron-founding industry which prospered from the 14th century until it was superseded by Northern-based coal-fired smelting in the 18th century. Indeed, this now-tranquil area was once known as *"Thunderfield-in-the-Forest"* because of the number of iron furnaces it contained.

The Seven Stars has been part of the landscape on Dawes Green in the village of Leigh for at least 300 years, although some locals

The Seven Stars

believe that to be a conservative figure and consider the pub to be more like five centuries old. What's a century or two, though, when you have found such a pleasant and welcoming country pub? Tables dot the sunny patio near the car park to the front of the pub, which has a neat, whitewashed and shingled exterior. The cosy bars inside are furnished in a country style, and the cheerful atmosphere reflects the pub's three (or is it five?) centuries of successfully catering to the needs of the locals. Jackie Doyle has run the pub for ten years and masterminds its excellent and comprehensive menu. She is also something of an expert on car rallying in the UK and Europe, so don't be surprised if the customer next to you opens a conversation in Finnish or Swedish. *The Seven Stars, Dawes Green, Bunce Common Road, Leigh, Reigate, Surrey RH2 8NS Tel: 01306 611254*

Horley

Map 4 ref I7

5 miles S of Reigate on the A23

The pleasant town of Horley lies on the Sussex border and not far from Gatwick Airport to the south. The proximity to the airport, surprisingly, has done little to alter the character of Horley although the town did undergo a transformation in the Victorian era after the arrival of the main railway line. The present arrangement of streets, set mostly in a gridiron pattern, branched out from the rail line to provide housing for railway workers and shops to cater to their needs. This neighbourhood, which constitutes most of the core of Horley, is trim and neat, and the overall effect is pleasant. Dotted among the 19th century buildings are a few survivors of earlier eras, including a lovely tile-hung cottage by the church.

The first unusual sign of ***Ye Olde Six Bells*** - six bells with walking sticks - is found at the end of Church Road directing visitors to this charming pub that has been serving Horley (and holy) locals for nearly a millennium. It is hard to date its origins precisely but legend has it that a secret passage links the pub to St Bartholomew's church next door, and the names of several 12th century priests can be found in the lobby. One very low roof timber has reputedly been dated as being 1,000 years old, so it is all the more fascinating to think that this venerable pub is the first experience many foreign visitors have of England. Gatwick Airport is close by, and pilots and airline passengers are among the varied clientele. Ye Olde Six Bells is tucked away on the outskirts of Horley and has a lovely setting on the banks of the River Mole.

Ye Olde Six Bells

A feature of this very interesting pub is the very large inglenook fireplace with its roaring log fire above which are the words *"keep me alive and I'll keep you warm"*. A large bay-window provides beautiful views of the weeping willow trees which are a feature of the pleasant riverside garden. The pub has a menu catering for a wide range of tastes. Customers can work up an appetite reading the newspapers and magazines provided by the pub or playing boules outside in the garden where there is ample room to sit and enjoy the riverside view. *Ye Olde Six Bells, Church Road, Horley, Surrey RH6 8AD Tel: 01293 783792*

East to the Kent Border

Bletchingley *Map 4 ref I6*

3 miles E of Reigate on the A25

Bletchingley is a highly picturesque village and former *"rotten borough"* which once had its own castle and street market. Traces of the Norman fortification thought to have been built by Richard de

Tonbridge in the 12th century can be seen in the grounds of ***Castle Hill***, a private house lying to the south of the A25. Closer to the centre, the old market in Middle Row is an exceptionally lovely thoroughfare which, like the nearby High Street, contains some wonderful old timber-framed and tile-hung houses and cottages.

Some fine early buildings can also be found in ***Church Walk***, the lane leading to Bletchingley's Perpendicular church of ***St Mary***. The oldest part of this sizeable sandstone structure, the Norman west tower, dates from the end of the 11th century; it had a spire until a bolt of lightning destroyed it in 1606. Inside, there is a 13th century hermit's cell, a wonderful assortment of mediaeval gargoyles, a 16th century monumental brass of a local tanner and his wife, and an extravagant sculpted monument to Sir Robert Clayton, a City money lender and former Lord Mayor of London who died in 1707. The church also contains the sizeable tomb of Sir Thomas Cawarden, the former owner of Bletchingley Place, who acquired the manor house from Anne of Cleves after she had won it from Henry VIII in her divorce settlement.

A couple of interesting settlements lie within easy reach of Bletchingley. ***Pendell***, a two-minute drive to the northwest, contains the striking Jacobean-style ***Pendell Court***, which was built in 1624, and the neoclassical ***Pendell House***, which was built twelve years later on an adjacent site. Brewer Street, one mile to the north, contains the remains of Anne of Cleves' manor house; this was remodelled in the 18th century and is now known as Place Farm.

Outwood *Map 4 ref I7*

5 miles SE of Reigate off the M23

Although Outwood is accessible from the M23 a more pleasant approach leads southwards from Bletchingley along a country road across the Weald. ***Outwood Common***, the area of high ground to the east of village, is best known for being the location of one of the most interesting windmills in the country.

The Post Mill is acknowledged as the oldest working windmill in England. It was built in 1665 and it is said that from the top of the mill, some 39 feet up, the Great Fire of London was visible 27 miles away. Unlike other ancient buildings in England, the Post Mill's early history is not shrouded in mystery and conjecture: it was built by Thomas Budgen, a miller of Nutfield, and the original deeds are still in existence.

The term "post mill" describes the structure and mechanism of this remarkable building. The whole body of the mill, including its sails and machinery, balances on a huge central post. This post is made from oak which, it is said, was drawn seven miles by oxcart from Crabbet Park, near Crawley, where it was felled. It is supported by four diagonal quarter bars and two crosstrees; these in turn rest on four brick piers. The purpose of this post system is to allow the mill to be turned to face the breeze; it is so finely balanced that a single person can turn the sails into the wind.

The Post Mill

Another special design feature incorporated around 100 years later allows the angle of the sails to be adjusted to suit different wind conditions using a system of elliptical springs.

For over a century, a second "smock" windmill stood nearby, and the pair were known as the Cat and Fiddle; sadly, the Fiddle blew down in a storm in the early 1960s.

You can learn all about the mill's operation and history from its owner, Sheila Thomas, who is a mine of information not only about the Post Mill but about Outwood itself. Visitors are invited to tour the various floors of the mill, learning along the way how the speed of the grinding can be adjusted according to wind speed and how the wholemeal is ground and stored. You can wander freely among the ducks, hens and geese around the mill, which is surrounded by common land and National Trust woodland where there are nature walks and good spots for picnics. *The Post Mill, Outwood Common, Outwood, Surrey RH1 5PW Tel: 01342 843644*

Burstow

Map 4 ref I7

8 miles SE of Reigate off the B2037

The lanes to the south of Outwood lead through Smallfield to Burstow, a well-kept village whose church, ***St Bartholomew's***,

St Bartholomew's Church, Burstow

has a surprisingly well preserved late mediaeval timber-framed tower. This hefty 15th century structure supports a peal of six bells, the largest of which weighs over half a ton. The church itself is an attractive mixture of Norman, Perpendicular, and Victorian influences; the chancel contains the remains of John Flamsteed, a former rector and the first Astronomer Royal, who is best remembered for his maps of the night skies which were compiled in the late 17th century as an aid to marine navigation.

About one mile north of Burstow is ***Smallfield Place***, regarded by many as the best example of a stone-built country home in Surrey. Its almost forbidding appearance is at odds with the mellow brick or aged timber exteriors of so many Surrey manor houses. The house was built at the beginning of the 17th century and presents a long, largely unadorned two-storey Wealden stone face to the curious public.

Lingfield

Map 4 ref J7

12 miles SE of Reigate off the A22

Lingfield is a large village which is set within delightful wooded countryside in the southeastern corner of the county. Almost large enough to be called a town, "leafy Lingfield" is perhaps best known to the world at large for its ***racecourse***. However, the settlement has long been an important agricultural centre whose largely Perpendicular church of ***St Peter and St Paul*** has been enlarged over the centuries to create what has become known as the *"Westminster Abbey of Surrey"*. As well as having a rare double nave and an exceptional collection of monumental brasses, the church also contains a surprising number of memorials to members of the Cobham

Monument, Lingfield Church

family, the medieval lords of the manor who lived at the now demolished Starborough Castle, a mile and a half to the east. Each of the first four barons has a sizeable tomb showing an effigy of its occupant; these date between 1361 and 1471 and are particularly fascinating to those with an interest in the development of late-medieval armour over this period.

The broad thoroughfare leading down from the church is lined with characteristic weatherboarded and tile-fronted buildings, including Pollard Cottage, with its unusual 15th century shop front, the 16th century Old Town Stores, and the Star Inn Cottages, built around 1700. The country library on the opposite side of the church is a former farmhouse which was built in the 17th century on the site of a Carthusian college founded in the 1400's by Sir Reginald Cobham. Elsewhere in Lingfield, a couple of interesting features can be found near the pond in Plaistow Street: the 15th century village cross and the old lock-up, a small local gaol which was built in 1772 and in use until 1882.

Along the edge of Lingfield lies Common Road and on it you can find ***The Hare and Hounds***, an unspoilt nineteenth century pub with a good range of beers and ales as well as an imaginative choice of freshly prepared food. Owner Simon Sheasby takes a great deal of pride in the appearance of the pub - which manages to be bright in the summer yet cosy in the winter - as well as the food it offers. His own wide travels have made him sympathetic to the needs of the most exacting of customers. This is the sort of pub where your meal is cooked from scratch rather than kept warm for hours on

The Hare and Hounds

end. Picnic tables outside offer the chance to watch passers-by on the Common Road, including those going to or from the races at Lingfield racecourse. Race days are popular at the Hare and Hounds, and it's never hard to tell who is celebrating a big win and who is regretting that last big bet. *The Hare and Hounds, Common Road, Lingfield, Surrey RH7 6BZ Tel: 01342 832351*

Greathed Manor, to the southeast of Lingfield, is a substantial Victorian manor house built in 1868 for the Spender Clay family. Haxted Mill, 2 miles to the northeast of Lingfield, is a working late 17th century water mill which also contains an informative mill museum; exhibits include machinery, equipment and artefacts relating to the history of water-power.

Architectural historians cannot agree on whether ***The Blue Anchor*** at Blindley Heath dates from the 16th or the 15th century, although some place it even earlier - being built as part of Godstone Manor in the late 13th century. A look inside offers proof enough of its long history. Wooden beams, church pew seats and three log fires - including a lovely inglenook fireplace - create a sense of cosiness in what is in fact a very roomy interior. Old prints and photographs line the walls and dried flower displays add dashes of colour throughout.

The Blue Anchor

The pub has copies of the daily newspapers for the use of customers, adding a Continental touch to a pub that could hardly be more English, with its hand-pulled real ales and conversations about cricket. The Blue Anchor has an extensive menu, with meals to suit every appetite. Gardens front and back, with the bonus of a duck pond in front, make sunny spots for eating and drinking, and many local stable girls simply tie their horses outside when they arrive. A large car park caters to those who arrive on four wheels. Ramblers use the Blue Anchor as a base for walks in the nearby countryside. *The Blue Anchor, Blindley Heath, Lingfield, Surrey RH7 6JJ Tel: 01342 832017*

Haxted

Map 4 ref K6

12 miles SE of Reigate off the B2039

Haxted is a pleasant hamlet on the Kent border, and the appearance of the houses shows the influence of Kent building styles. Weatherboarding, so often associated with Kent, features on many of the older houses alongside the more typically Surrey feature of tile-hung frontages. One of the larger weatherboard structures is ***Haxted Mill***, a water-mill built in the late 18th century. Seen alongside the tile-hung mill house next door the two buildings form a charming pair. Visitors can appreciate the mill's history by visiting the ***Haxted Watermill Museum*** housed inside.

Dormansland

Map 4 ref K7

12 miles SE of Reigate off the B2029

Dormansland presents itself as evidence for a bit of social history detective work. The cottages in this hamlet near the Sussex and Kent borders date from the Victorian era, with some 17th and 18th century examples mixed in. However, they share a common limitation - their size. Other Surrey hamlets have workmen's cottages but there is usually much more diversity in scale. Several social historians have proposed that these cottages were built by people who were squatting in common land.

Just outside the village is an altogether grander structure, ***Old Surrey Hall***, built in 1450 on the remote border with Sussex. Much of the 15th century section, with its close timbering exterior, survives, but the overall moated quadrangle of today's house dates from 1922, representing a renovation work of near genius by the architect George Crawley.

Crowhurst

Map 4 ref J6

1 mile SE of Reigate off the A22

Crowhurst contains a 1,000 year old yew tree whose branches are said to enclose an area over 30 feet in diameter; during the 1820's, a covered cafe was formed by removing some of the central branches and installing tables and chairs. Crowhurst Place, to the south-west, was rebuilt after the First World War on the site of a 15th century moated manor house.

Limpsfield

Map 4 ref K5

9 miles E of Reigate on the B269

The churchyard at Limpsfield, three miles to the east of Godstone, contains the grave of the composer, Frederick Delius, who despite having died in France, left instructions that he should be buried in an English country graveyard. ***Detillens***, a rare 15th century "hall" house, is also located in Limpsfield. This striking building has an unusual "king-post" roof, and despite having been given a new facade in the 18th century, is a good example of a house belonging to a Surrey yeoman, a member of the class of small freeholders who cultivated their own land; inside, there is an interesting collection of period furniture, china and militaria.

Limpsfield Chart, or simply The Chart, constitutes a hilltop common with some lovely views eastwards across Kent. Next to the common is a 17th century ***Mill House***; the windmill itself was removed in 1925. Elsewhere in The Chart there are handsome groupings of stone-built houses, cottages, and farm buildings, best exemplified by the ensemble at Moorhouse Farm.

The fine walking country around Limpsfield Chart, on the Surrey border with Kent, is the setting for ***The Carpenters Arms***, a handsome country pub set right on the edge of the village and just a few paces from some of the best walks in the area. Walkers can choose between scaling the 900 foot Downs to the north of the village or meandering through the extensive woodland to the east. The pub name derives from its original role as the village carpen-

The Carpenters Arms

ter's shop, and there is a good, solid feel about the place. Glen and Joanne Trew are friendly landlords, and their Sunday lunch is so popular that it is advisable to book ahead. There is a good range of ales, beers and lagers and in warmer weather customers benefit from one of the largest pub gardens in the county - ideal for soaking up the rural feel of the pub and the village. *The Carpenters Arms, 12 Tally Road, Limpsfield Chart, Oxted, Surrey RH8 0TG*

Oxted *Map 4 ref J5*

8 miles E of Reigate off the A25

Oxted is an old town that prospered because of its position just below the Downs and consequently a good trading link with the rest of Surrey. Today, however, Oxted constitutes two distinct parts. New

Oxted lies between the original town and Limpsfield to the east; it grew up around the railway station which was built in the 19th century. Old Oxted is also largely Victorian to the eye, but occasionally the visitor notices some survivors of earlier centuries such as the ***Forge House*** and ***Beam Cottages***, with their medieval core and 17th century exteriors. Streeters Cottage, built in the 17th century, presents a large timber-framed gable to the road.

If you could peel off the outer layers of ***The George Inn***, a traditional pub which lies in the heart of Old Oxted, you would uncover layer upon layer of history. Most of the visible exterior dates from a late eighteenth-century face-lift when a brick facade was laid over the original timber framing. This framing, now mostly hidden, would

The George Inn

tell the tale of a pub with a history dating back to the fifteenth century. Savour a pint and admire the leaded windows and heavy medieval floor joists and ask manager Mikki Tibbs for more clues about the five centuries of inn-keeping that the inn represents. It's not all architectural history at the George, however. Its reputation as a popular pub with locals as well as walkers stems from the range of real ales and the hearty meals served. There are vegetarian meals, fish dishes, salads and quiches, but somehow it seems appropriate to have a traditional English steak in such a setting - the menu offers no fewer than eight steak alternatives. *The George Inn, High Street, Old Oxted, Surrey RH8 9LP Tel: 01883 713453*

The Chart is the home of ***Joyces on the Chart***, a memorable tea room that also serves light lunches and occasional evening meals. It has a lovely location in the Chart, a charming little village near

Joyces on the Chart

Oxted, full of stone-built cottages and sunny gardens. Such a setting is defiantly uncommercial, and Joyces on the Chart - which also has an amazing selection of greetings cards - is the last remaining shop still open in this village. It's not hard to understand its staying power. The setting is romantic, with its handsome awning announcing its presence. Inside is some of the best-cooked food available for miles around, ranging from home-made soups and broths to steak, seafood and vegetarian specialities. For many of its repeat customers, though, the high point is the traditional cream tea or simply a good filter coffee accompanied by a rock bun, Danish pastry or home-made cake. The garden is a tranquil oasis from the world's cares. *Joyces on the Chart, Post Office Row, The Chart, Oxted, Surrey RH8 0TH Tel: 01883 722195*

Staffhurst Wood — *Map 4 ref J6*

8 miles E of Reigate off the A25

In the attractive village of Staffhurst Wood near Oxted and close to the Kent border lies ***The Royal Oak***. On the outside it is the quintessential English pub, with leafy vines trailing down the shingled upper storey and a timber-frame gable. Tables, a children's play

The Royal Oak

area and a spacious patio are geared to summer barbecues and there are views over three counties - Sussex being the third. Inside is a lovely marriage of English and French cultures, with real ale, darts and open fires setting the scene for a Gallic-inspired menu. Sondrine Costanzo and Sebastien Gayet learned the trade in their native France and have been manager and chef of the Royal Oak since 1994. Specialities such as moules marinieres, paupiette of guinea fowl and pan-fried pork fillet Normandie have a distinctly cross-Channel flavour. The best of British is also represented with roast duck, smoked chicken salad and pan-fried red mullet. An imaginative selection of wines, including some inspired New World choices, rounds off an excellent meal. *The Royal Oak, Staffhurst Wood, Oxted, Surrey RH8 0RR Tel 01833 722207*

Godstone

Map 4 ref J5

6 miles E of Reigate off the A22

Although Godstone is now thankfully bypassed by the A22, the A25 east-west route still passes through its heart, making a sharp change in direction as it does so. Fortunately, the village manages to endure the periodic onslaught of traffic and indeed, its Tudor and Elizabethan character has survived relatively intact. Godstone's most distinguished building, the White Hart Inn in the High Street, claims to have been visited by Richard II, Elizabeth I, Queen Victoria, and even the Tsar of Russia who broke his journey here in 1815. A series of attractive lanes and alleyways connects the High Street to the village green, a broad open space with a cricket pitch which is surrounded by a wonderful collection of 16th and 17th century buildings, including the Tudor-built Hare and Hounds Inn.

Godstone's parish church of ***St Nicholas*** is situated half a mile east of the centre and can be reached from the White Hart along an old thoroughfare known as Bay Path. Although Norman in origin, the building was virtually rebuilt in the 1870s by Sir George Gilbert Scott, a local resident at the time. Inside, there is a marble memorial to a cousin of John Evelyn, the famous 17th century diarist. The area around the church contains some fine old buildings, including a row of 19th century almshouses and the 16th century timber-framed ***Old Pack House***, which lies a short distance away to the south. Bay Path also leads to a former hammer pond, ***Bay Pond***, which is now a designated nature reserve. At one time, its water would have been used to power the mechanical hammers in a nearby iron foundry, an indication of Godstone's lost industrial past which also included the manufacture of gunpowder and leatherware.

Godstone Farm, in Tilburstow Hill Road to the south of the village, is an open farm where children can experience life on the farm at first hand.

Tourist Information Centres

Surrey is part of the South East England Tourist Information Centre Network. Each centre, or TIC, provides a wide range of services, including accommodation booking, local events information, travel information and an extensive selection of maps, guides, and brochures. The two Surrey TICs, like other centres in the network, can provide detailed information on the area within a 50 mile radius. They operate accommodation booking services for their local area and, through the other Tourist Information Centres in the Network, onward into other parts of the region and country.

Centres in **bold** are open all the year around.

Farnham

Vernon House, 28 West Street, Farnham, Surrey GU9 7DR
Tel: 01252 715109, Fax: 01252 717377

Guildford

14 Tunsgate, Guildford, Surrey GU1 3QT
Tel: 01483 444333, Fax: 01483 302046

Index

D

E

F

G

H

K

L

M

S

T

U

V

W

Y

The Hidden Places Series

ORDER FORM

To order more copies of this title or any of the others in this series please complete the order form below and send to:

Travel Publishing Ltd,7a Apollo House, Calleva Park Aldermaston, Berkshire, RG7 8TN

	Price	Quantity	Value
Regional Titles			
Channel Islands	£6.99	....	....
Devon & Cornwall	£4.95	....	....
Dorset, Hants & Isle of Wight	£4.95	....	....
East Anglia	£4.95	....	....
Gloucestershire	£6.99	....	....
Heart of England	£4.95	....	....
Lancashire & Cheshire	£4.95	....	....
Lake District & Cumbria	£4.95	....	....
Northeast Yorkshire	£6.99	....	....
Northumberland & Durham	£6.99	....	....
Nottinghamshire	£6.99	....	....
Peak District	£6.99	....	....
Potteries	£6.99	....	....
Somerset	£6.99	....	....
South East	£4.95	....	....
South Wales	£4.95	....	....
Surrey	£6.99	....	....
Sussex	£6.99	....	....
Thames & Chilterns	£5.99	....	....
Welsh Borders	£5.99	....	....
Wiltshire	£6.99	....	....
Yorkshire Dales	£6.99	....	....
Set of any 5 Regional titles	**£25.00**	....	....
National Titles			
England	£9.99	....	....
Ireland	£8.99	....	....
Scotland	£8.99	....	....
Wales	£8.99	....	....
Set of all 4 National titles	**£28.00**	....	....
	TOTAL	______	______

For orders of less than 4 copies please add £1 per book for postage & packing. Orders over 4 copies P & P free.

PLEASE TURN OVER TO COMPLETE PAYMENT DETAILS

The Hidden Places Series
ORDER FORM

Please complete following details:

I wish to pay for this order by:

Cheque:	☐	Switch:	☐
Access:	☐	Visa:	☐

Either:

Card No: ☐☐☐☐ ☐☐☐☐ ☐☐☐☐ ☐☐☐☐

Expiry Date: ☐☐ ☐☐

Signature: ....

Or:

I enclose a cheque for £ .... made payable to Travel Publishing Ltd

NAME: ....

ADDRESS: ....

....

....

....

POSTCODE: ....

TEL NO: ....

Please send to: Travel Publishing Ltd
7a Apollo House
Calleva Park
Aldermaston
Berkshire, RG7 8TN

The Hidden Places Series

READER REACTION FORM

The Hidden Places research team would like to receive reader's comments on any visitor attractions or places reviewed in the book and also recommendations for suitable entries to be included in the next edition. This will help ensure that the ***Hidden Places*** series continues to provide its readers with useful information on the more interesting, unusual or unique features of each attraction or place ensuring that their stay in the local area is an enjoyable and stimulating experience.

To provide your comments or recommendations would you please complete the forms below as indicated and send to: **The Research Department, Travel Publishing Ltd., 7a Apollo House, Calleva Park, Aldermaston, Reading, RG7 8TN.**

Please tick as appropriate: Comments ☐ Recommendation ☐

Name of *"Hidden Place"*:

Address:

Telephone Number:

Name of Contact:

Comments/Reason for recommendation:

Name of Reader:

Address:

Telephone Number:

The Hidden Places Series

READER REACTION FORM

The Hidden Places research team would like to receive reader's comments on any visitor attractions or places reviewed in the book and also recommendations for suitable entries to be included in the next edition. This will help ensure that the ***Hidden Places*** series continues to provide its readers with useful information on the more interesting, unusual or unique features of each attraction or place ensuring that their stay in the local area is an enjoyable and stimulating experience.

To provide your comments or recommendations would you please complete the forms below as indicated and send to: **The Research Department, Travel Publishing Ltd., 7a Apollo House, Calleva Park, Aldermaston, Reading, RG7 8TN.**

Please tick as appropriate: Comments ☐ Recommendation ☐

Name of *"Hidden Place"*:

Address:

Telephone Number:

Name of Contact:

Comments/Reason for recommendation:

Name of Reader:

Address:

Telephone Number:

The Hidden Places Series

READER REACTION FORM

The Hidden Places research team would like to receive reader's comments on any visitor attractions or places reviewed in the book and also recommendations for suitable entries to be included in the next edition. This will help ensure that the ***Hidden Places*** series continues to provide its readers with useful information on the more interesting, unusual or unique features of each attraction or place ensuring that their stay in the local area is an enjoyable and stimulating experience.

To provide your comments or recommendations would you please complete the forms below as indicated and send to: **The Research Department, Travel Publishing Ltd., 7a Apollo House, Calleva Park, Aldermaston, Reading, RG7 8TN.**

Please tick as appropriate: Comments ☐ Recommendation ☐

Name of *"Hidden Place"*:

Address:

Telephone Number:

Name of Contact:

Comments/Reason for recommendation:

Name of Reader:

Address:

Telephone Number:

The Hidden Places Series

READER REACTION FORM

The Hidden Places research team would like to receive reader's comments on any visitor attractions or places reviewed in the book and also recommendations for suitable entries to be included in the next edition. This will help ensure that the ***Hidden Places*** series continues to provide its readers with useful information on the more interesting, unusual or unique features of each attraction or place ensuring that their stay in the local area is an enjoyable and stimulating experience.

To provide your comments or recommendations would you please complete the forms below as indicated and send to: **The Research Department, Travel Publishing Ltd., 7a Apollo House, Calleva Park, Aldermaston, Reading, RG7 8TN.**

Please tick as appropriate: Comments ☐ Recommendation ☐

Name of *"Hidden Place"*:

Address:

Telephone Number:

Name of Contact:

Comments/Reason for recommendation:

Name of Reader:

Address:

Telephone Number:

Map Section

The following pages of maps encompass the main cities, towns and geographical features of Surrey, as well as all the many interesting places featured in the guide. Distances are indicated by the use of scale bars located below each of the maps

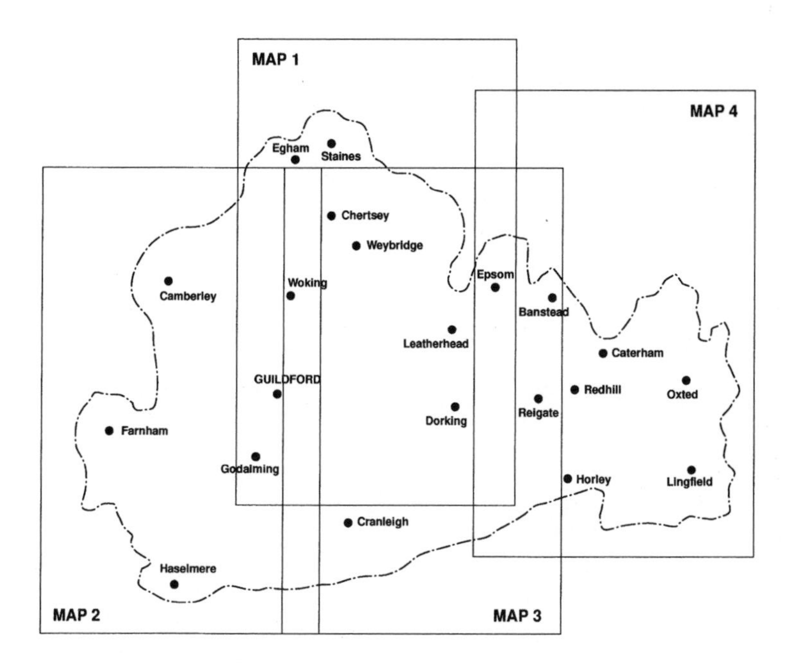

These maps are small scale extracts from the *Sussex & Surrey Official Tourist Map,* reproduced with kind permission of *Estates Publications*.

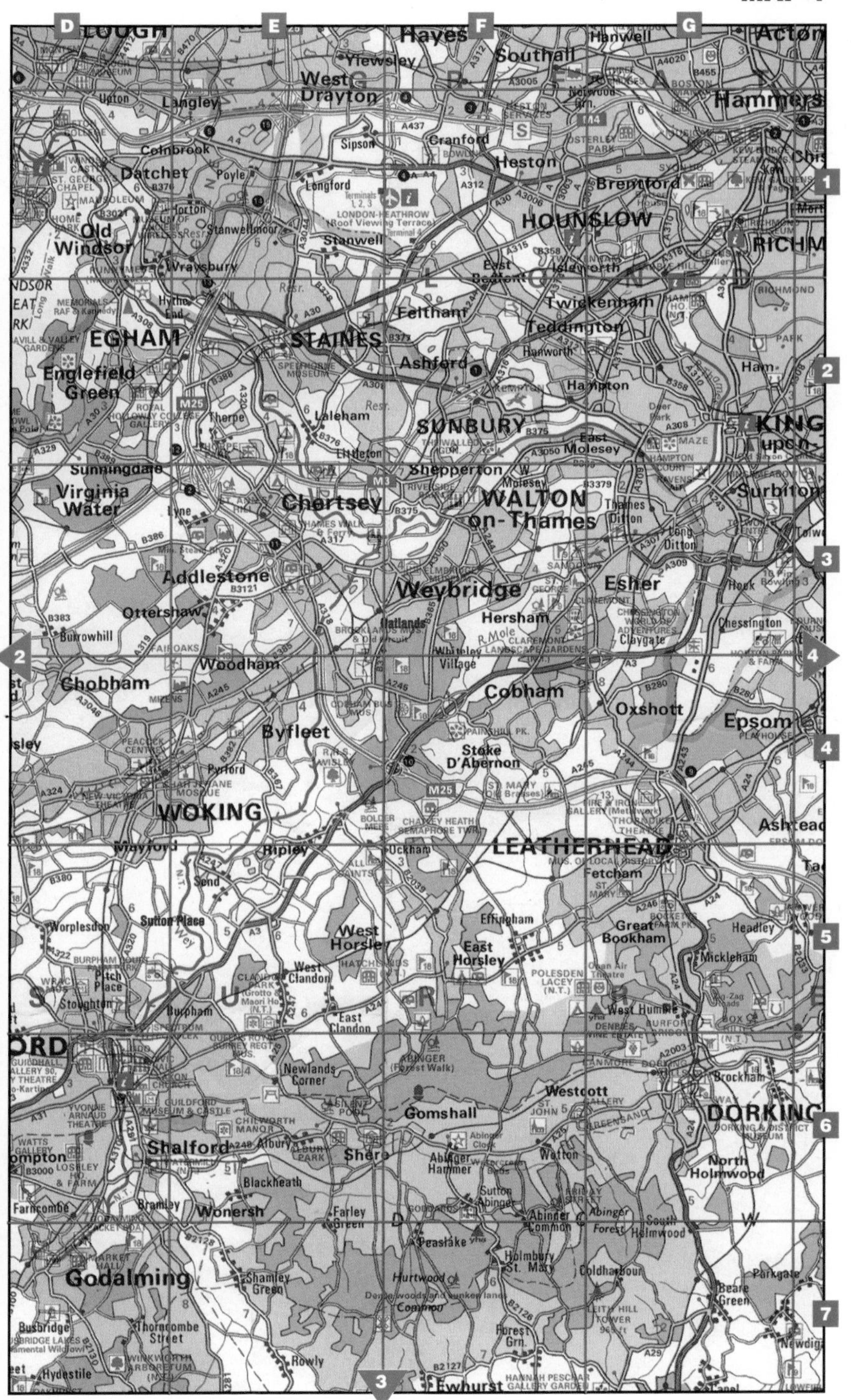

0 1 2 3 4 5 miles
0 1 2 3 4 5 6 7 8 kilometres

©Estate Publications Crown Copyright Reserved

MAP 2

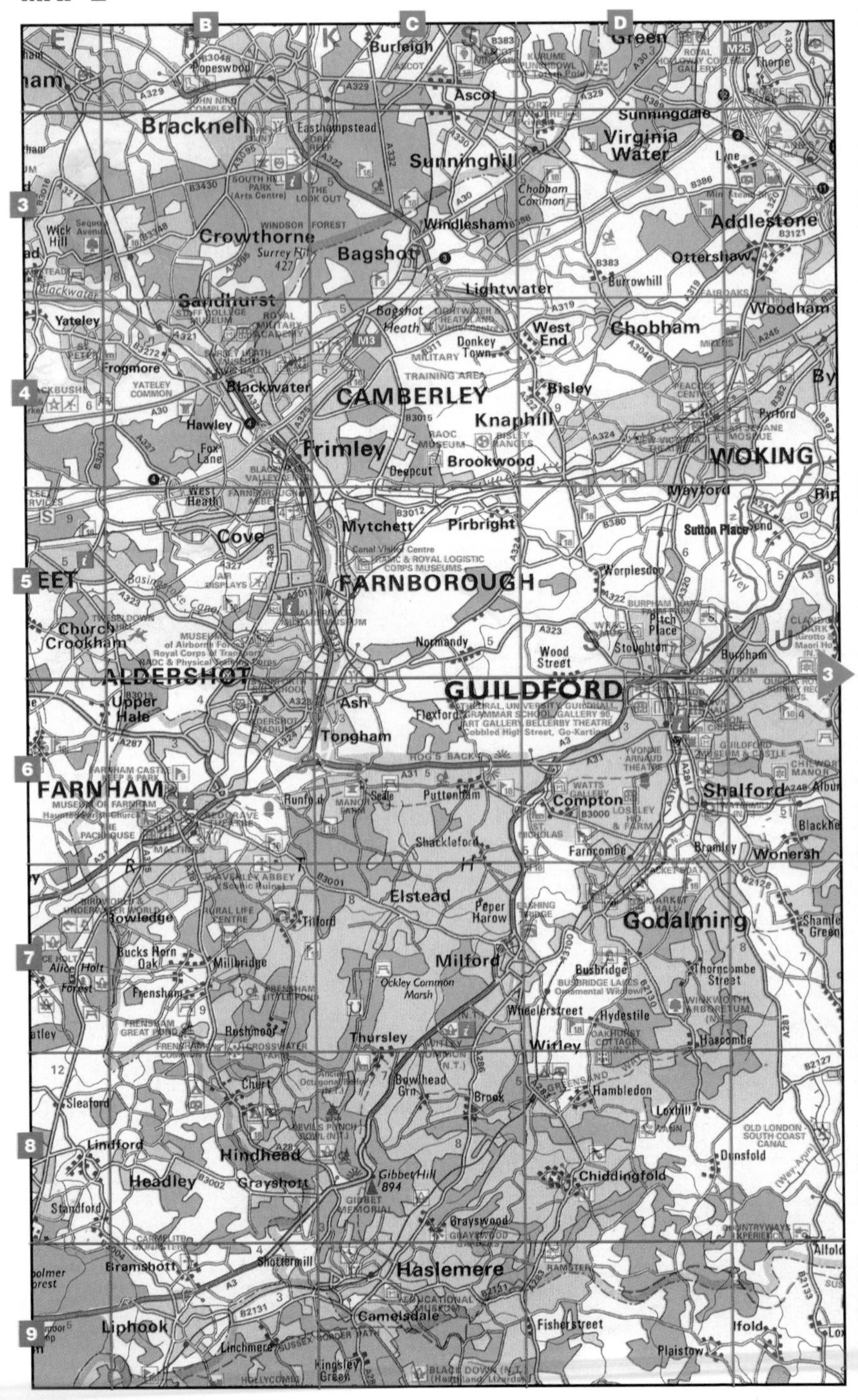

©Estate Publications Crown Copyright Reserved

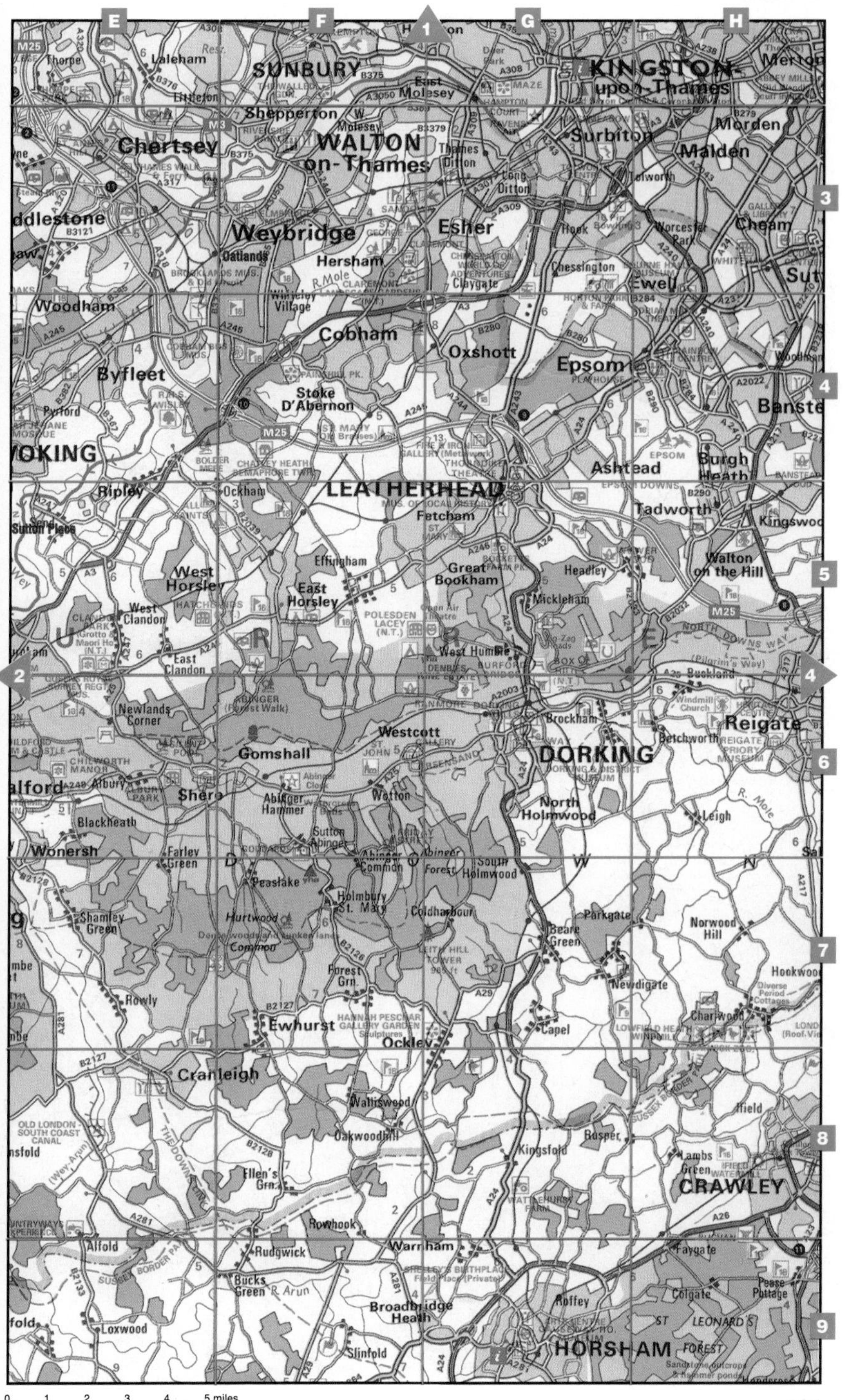
SUNBURY
KINGSTON-upon-Thames
Laleham
Thorpe
Littleton
East Molesey
Shepperton
Chertsey
WALTON on-Thames
Thames Ditton
Surbiton
Morden
Malden
Long Ditton
Tolworth
Addlestone
Weybridge
Oatlands
Esher
Hook
Worcester Park
Cheam
Hersham
Whiteley Village
Claygate
Chessington
Ewell
Woodham
Cobham
Oxshott
Epsom
Byfleet
Stoke D'Abernon
Pyrford
WOKING
Ashtead
Burgh Heath
Ripley
Ockham
LEATHERHEAD
Fetcham
Tadworth
Kingswood
Send
Sutton Place
West Horsley
Effingham
East Horsley
Great Bookham
Headley
Walton on the Hill
West Clandon
East Clandon
Mickleham
West Humble
Buckland
Newlands Corner
Brockham
Reigate
Westcott
Gomshall
DORKING
Betchworth
Albury
Shere
Abinger Hammer
Wotton
North Holmwood
Leigh
Blackheath
Wonersh
Farley Green
Sutton Abinger
Abinger Common
South Holmwood
Peaslake
Holmbury St. Mary
Coldharbour
Shamley Green
Beare Green
Parkgate
Norwood Hill
Forest Grn.
Newdigate
Hookwood
Rowly
Ewhurst
Ockley
Capel
Charlwood
Cranleigh
Walliswood
Ifield
Oakwoodhill
Rusper
Kingsfold
Lambs Green
CRAWLEY
Ellen's Grn.
Rowhook
Alfold
Rudgwick
Warnham
Faygate
Bucks Green
Colgate
Pease Pottage
Roffey
Broadbridge Heath
Loxwood
Slinfold
HORSHAM
M25
M3
A3
A24
A25
A29
A281
A246
A243
A217
0 1 2 3 4 5 miles
0 1 2 3 4 5 6 7 8 kilometres

MAP 4

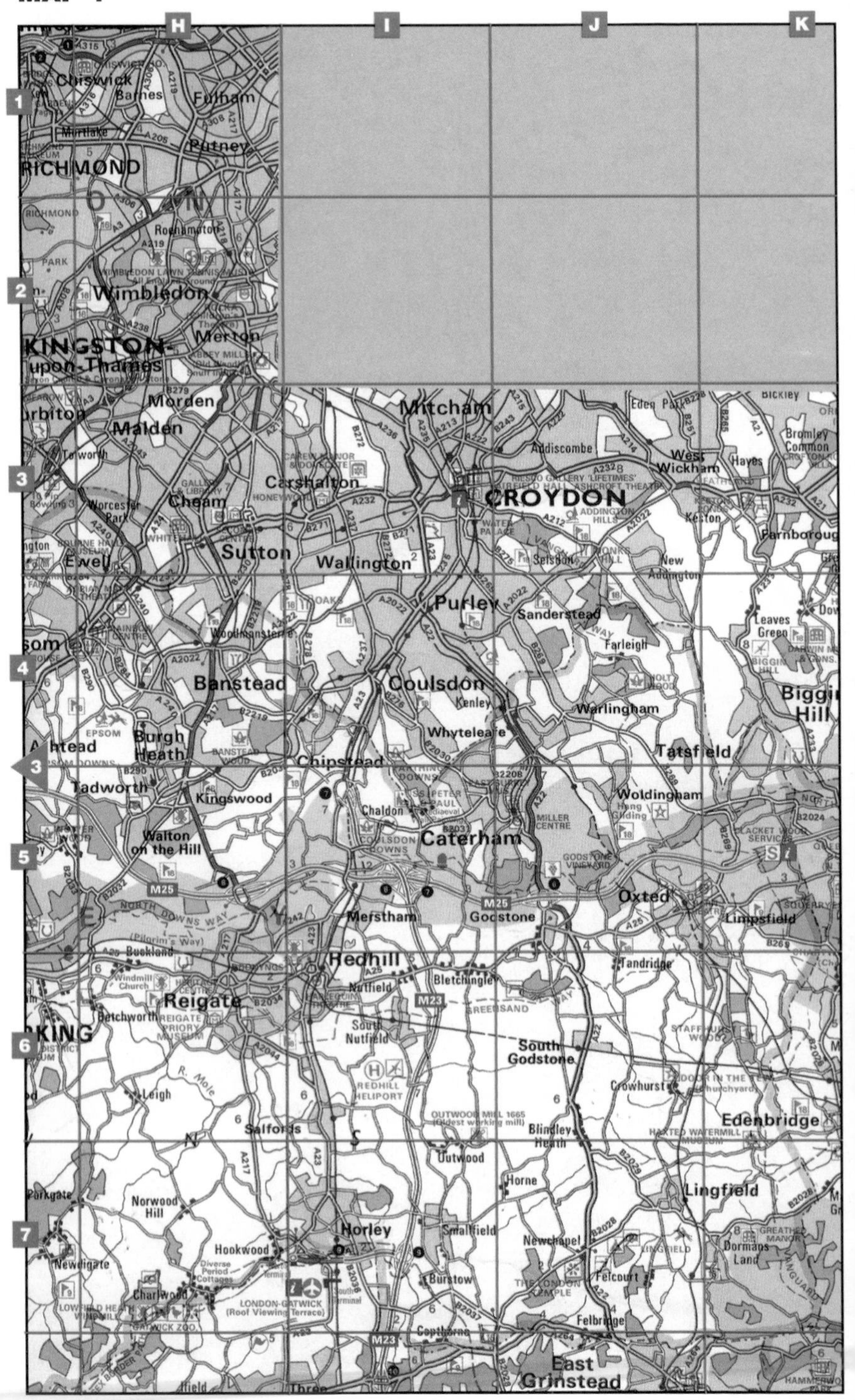

 ©Estate Publications Crown Copyright Reserved

0 1 2 3 4 5 miles
0 1 2 3 4 5 6 7 8 kilometres